Joey Asher

# Even a  Geek  Can Speak

## Low-Tech Presentation Skills for High-Tech People

Persuasive
Speaker
Press

Atlanta, Georgia

Published by
Persuasive Speaker Press
Atlanta, Georgia

Printed in Canada

3rd printing 2008

Library of Congress Catalog Card Number: 00-105150

978-0-9785776-0-5

Jacket and book design by Claire Newbury

Persuasive Speaker Press® is a registered trademark of
Speechworks/Asher Communications, Inc.
3500 Piedmont Road, Suite 330
Atlanta, Georgia 30305

*To my beloved, geeky household:*
*Johanna, Benjamin, Elliott, and Annie.*

# Even a
# Geek
# Can Speak

# CONTENTS

# CONTENTS

# Is There Some Geek in Your Speak?

**This is a book for geeks who speak.**
While this book will show you how to eliminate geeky jargon, more importantly it will show you how to speak simply about complex things.

**For example, this book will help you:**
- Sell the latest Hitachi Data Systems data storage system to the Delta Air Lines board of directors and chief information officer.
- Explain in simple terms to a meeting of upper-level managers why the skew in the current curve makes diode transistor logic superior to *transistor* transistor logic.
- Deliver the keynote address at the World Energy Engineering Conference.

- Explain to your client why she should reengineer the logistical process for delivering widgets from the warehouse to the factory door.
- Help a non-tekkie CEO understand why she cannot go another day without your company's new accounting software.
- Woo investors in a new high-tech start-up that is going to make you the next high-tech gazillionaire.
- Schmooze at a cocktail party so that when someone asks you, "So, Joey, what do you do?" your response does not label you "nerd" for the rest of the party.

**And if you don't work in a "high-tech" job but you still need to talk simply about complex things, this book will help you too. For example, this book will help:**

* **Tax lawyers** keep their clients from keeling over when listening to how the changes in the tax code will affect their business.
* **Accountants** persuade their fellow accountants of the need to make a change to the GAAP (Generally Accepted Accounting Principles).
* **Financial analysts** explain that the latest quarterly reports mean it's time to dump all Brazilian telecommunications stock.
* **Environmental consultants** explain the process for cleaning up the local river basin.
* **Real estate appraisers** explain to lawyers what they need to know about property evaluation.

**It's cool to be a geek. But it's not cool to speak like one: Take the Geek Speak Assessment Test**

It's cool to be a geek. Geeks know how everything actually works. Geeks rule! Look at Bill Gates – he has more money than most countries. When I was practicing law and representing electric companies, I was proud to be called a "utility geek."

But the only way to be a cool geek is to be able to speak with clarity and poise about your area of expertise. With that in mind, take the Geek Speak Assessment Test (GSAT). Answer all questions by circling "yes" or "no."

- Whenever I speak to others about what I've been working on at the office, people look at me with a puzzled smile, like maybe I'm one of those little yipping peek-a-poo dogs or maybe the teacher in the old Peanuts cartoons whose voice sounds like a trumpet with a "Wah, wah" mute. **Yes No**
- Whenever I go on a sales call, I start by whipping out an Excel spreadsheet and taking my prospect through the "specs, stats, and financials" – all of which, I explain to my customer, are subject to change "depending on the number of mods." **Yes No**
- I consider myself a "person of substance" who believes in giving people facts only and letting them make conclusions themselves. **Yes No**
- I regularly use jargon like "paradigm," "liquidity event," or "adaptive correlation engine." **Yes No**
- I grumble frequently about the sales and marketing guys and gals on the fifteenth floor. Sure, they're great looking and very friendly, but they don't really have a clue about the inner workings of our company's products. **Yes No**
- Even though my new software program will make anyone who uses it rich, thin, and sexually gratified with absolutely no effort, my PowerPoint presentation leaves venture capitalists unsure about whether anyone might want my product. **Yes No**
- I speak in the soft, dull monotone of a person who has spent three weeks in my cubicle debugging a complex economic computer model. **Yes No**
- I have used the following words in conversation: "A recent amendment to the Federal Tax Code requires that you ..." (substitute any words you want for the words "Federal Tax"). **Yes No**
- I take a Hewlett-Packard scientific calculator with me when I go to a meeting or sales call because I find that others like it when I take it out and use it during my presentations. **Yes No**
- I begin many of my presentations with the following words: "Could someone please dim the lights? O.K. This first slide is about. . . ." **Yes No**

### Self-Scoring GSAT Scale:

**0-3 Yeses:** Mild Geek Speaker. You may suffer from a mild form of geek speak. It shouldn't take too much effort for you to learn to articulate your ideas. And when you do, you will probably be able to rise to the top of your industry with little trouble. **Diagnosis: Read on.**

**4-7 Yeses:** Generally Incomprehensible Geek Speaker. People generally have no clue what you're talking about. They listen to you and think to themselves, "He must be smart." If you can learn to articulate your ideas, your colleagues and friends will begin saying, "He *is* smart." More importantly, if you cure your geek speak tendencies, you probably will get a raise. **Diagnosis: Read on.**

**8-10 Yeses:** Totally Incomprehensible Geek Speaker. Starting a conversation with you is a little like taking a swing at the tar baby. No matter how hard your listeners try, they can't get away from your never-ending stream of incomprehensible technical babble. And worse, you do not even begin to feel your listeners' pain. The great news, however, is that you know so much about your field that if you can learn to make others understand it, you're probably going to become filthy stinkin' rich. **Diagnosis: Read on.**

AND YOU'LL LEARN TO
SAY IT WITH STYLE

*Disturbing fact:* Only 7 percent of the impression that we geeks make when we communicate is based on what we say. On the other hand, 93 percent of the impression we make when we communicate is based on how we look and sound.

– Dr. Albert Mehrabian,
UCLA sociologist and
communications guru

### Great News for Geek Speakers

No matter what your score, the great news is that any geek can learn to articulate her ideas with clarity and style. To be sure, it takes practice. You're going to have to spend some time thinking about what your listeners really want to know from you. And you're going to have to consider the image you project. Do you come across as enthusiastic and exciting, or do you come across as a dull "tekkie nerd"? If you really want to change, this book will show you how.

Geek Speakers tend to communicate with all of the enthusiasm and style of a Lotus Spreadsheet. We see ourselves as people of sub-stance! Don't bother us with that style stuff. That's for used-car salesmen. We'd rather leave the pizzazz – the "wow" – to the marketing guys downtown. But the harsh reality is that style matters when we speak. This book shows how to speak with the kind of passion, excitement, and style that will ensure that people listen to your substance.

## Now Is the Time to De-Geek Your Speak

The need to learn to articulate complex ideas has never been greater. We see it in our workshops every week. So many of our clients must learn to articulate complex, often highly technical ideas: companies such as MCI Worldcom, INVESCO, Equifax, Scientific Atlanta, and Internet Security Systems. Even UPS no longer refers to itself as a truck com-pany, but rather as a "technology company with trucks."

And we meet so many people with wonderful ideas who have difficulty expressing those ideas. Charles Mosely, of Noro-Mosely Partners, sighs when he thinks of how often the high-tech pitches he hears are not clear, articulate presenta-tions but rather dry readings of what's on the presenter's PowerPoint slides. This book is the answer to those sighs.

So read on, my geek brothers and sisters. You have noth-ing to lose but your cubicles.

## PART I

*"Do me a favor, give me a formula
I can learn."*

**– Bob Baggerman, self-proclaimed geek, Georgia Tech
research engineer, and my neighbor**

# A Formula
# for De-Geeking
# Your Speak

So you're in your cubicle testing the assumptions of your economic model for projecting short-term sales for the Southeastern Power grid. The telephone rings and you answer. Someone has heard of your work and wants you to speak at an industry trade show next month. You say "yes" and hang up.

Now what?

You need to know how to put together a presentation. Ideally, this presentation will meet a few criteria. The presentation will:

- Show you off as an expert in your field.
- Convey your information in a clearly organized manner.
- Excite and motivate the audience.
- Be riveting and relevant.

I understand that in engineering school you probably didn't learn to put together a presentation. But chances are that you did spend a little time working with formulas of various types. The chapters in this section will show you a very effective formula to help you put together a presentation that will make sure you achieve your goals.

## CHAPTER 1

*"Off the cuff is off the mark."*
**– Speechworks**

# The Speechworks Formula

You will be glad to know, my fellow geeks, that there is a formula for clear communication. It is called the Speechworks Formula. It is a model for articulating complex ideas with simplicity. This Formula is as simple as booting up a computer. It's quicker than a T-1 line. And it's as reliable as any of Newton's theories.

And this Formula works for any situation where you have to communicate your ideas. You can use it to:

- Organize an address to the Comdex show.
- Formulate a report to the president of your bank on your progress with the new REIT initiative.
- Explain the tax code to your client.
- Persuade the president of Delta Air Lines to buy your company's new software product.
- Brief your boss on the progress of the lawsuit you're handling for the firm's biggest client.

## The Speechworks Formula

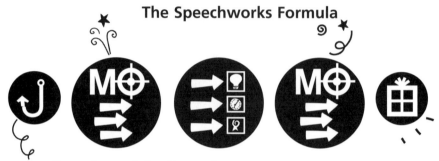

### Overview of the Formula

You will find the basics of all good spoken communication within the confines of this comfortable little Formula. Master it and your career prospects will soar. Fail to master its principles and . . . well . . . you may succeed anyway. But it won't be because you're a great geek communicator.

### Step One: Come Up with a Message Objective

Do this one thing consistently, my geek brothers and sisters, and you will be among the top 14 percent of communicators in the U.S. population. Why? Because never again will anyone say to you, "I'm not sure what your point is." With a good Message Objective ("MO"), you do the following:

**You form a clearly focused message that satisfies your listener's needs.**

Every time you put together a presentation, come up with an MO. Every time you think about what you're going to say at a meeting, come up with an MO. Every time you pick up the telephone to call a client, come up with an MO. Every time you write a letter, come up with an MO.

## Form the MO by bringing together two things:

**What you want.** Know what you want to accomplish with the communication. What do you want to happen as a result of what you're about to say? Do you want to persuade your client that you're right? Do you want to sell your boss on an idea? Do you want a prospect to buy your product?

**What's in it for the listener.** Determine what is in it for the listener. Remember that your listener is always wearing a headset tuned into his favorite radio station – WII-FM. What's In It For Me? What is it about your idea that will interest your boss? Does your boss want to save money for the department? What is it about your idea that will benefit your client? Does your client want to make sure that his product is installed on time? Why will your prospect benefit from this product? Will it make him richer, thinner or sexually more fulfilled?

### THE SEMISERIOUS SPEECHWORKS MO GUARANTEE.

The MO is the cornerstone of great persuasive communication. Master it, and Speechworks guarantees that you will achieve success in your field. In fact, if you fail to achieve success in your field despite consistent use of MOs in all communications, please send us your book and we'll gladly refund your money. Of course, we'll need examples of your last ten MOs. Please also define "success." If we think that your definition of success is unreasonable, then the deal is off. Also, send postage and a self-addressed stamped envelope for the refund check.

## Formulate the MO by bringing the two parts together.

The MO brings together what you want to accomplish with what your listener wants to accomplish. Formulate the MO as follows: "By [insert what you want to accomplish] you will [insert what your listener wants]."

Sample MOs include:

- By buying this computer program, your firm will save millions of dollars a year.
- By understanding this new tax law, you will better be able to advise your clients.
- When you cross your goal with the interest of the listener, you will be on target with your message.

- If you clean your room, I'll let you stay up to watch *The X-Files*.
- If you hire me, I'll bring in $100,000 in revenues in the first six months.
- By recommending our stock to your clients, you will be putting your clients in a position to make a lot of money.
- By understanding my ideas for a new flextime system, this company will gain access to a whole new pool of highly qualified employees.
- By following the ideas in this book, you will become among the best communicators in your industry.

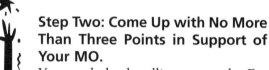

**TAKE THE SPEECHWORKS THREE-POINT PLEDGE.**

"I, [state your name], promise never to give more than three points in support of my MO for the rest of my life. So help me, Speechworks." If taking the three-point pledge during a group ceremony, it's traditional to shower your fellow inductees with cold champagne or that fizzy grape juice.

### Step Two: Come Up with No More Than Three Points in Support of Your MO.

You read the headline correctly. For the rest of your life, you need to limit yourself to no more than three points in support of your MO. Do this and you'll be among the top 8 percent of all communicators in North America. Most people throw out dozens of supporting points, most of which people never remember. Limit yourself to no more than three, and you're going to have impact.

"What about four points?" you ask.

Well, four would be one point too many.

Five?

That's two too many.

Six is . . . well, you get the idea.

**No more than three points – even for long presentations.** If you're giving a long presentation, you can still have three big points with lots of subpoints. But you need to organize your presentation around three big ideas that support your core MO.

## Step Three: Determine the Evidence to Support Each of Your Three Points and All Subpoints.

You need to support your points with evidence. The most exciting and usually most persuasive type of evidence is a relevant story. But you can also use personal examples, expert testimony, analogies, quotes, statistics, or other facts.

By the way, there's a term for people who make statements that they never support with evidence. They're called "blowhards." At Speechworks, we tell our clients that if they fail to support their claims with evidence, then those claims are nothing but "blah blah."

## Step Four: Determine Your Hook.

This is the grabber at the beginning of a presentation. A hook can be a fun fact, a relevant story, a quick analogy, or just a quick introduction. It doesn't have to be fancy. But it has to be quick and relevant to your presentation. Jokes are almost never good. Quotes work. So does a quick piece of expert testimony.

A hook might sound like this:

*Last year, 5,000 companies lost in excess of $1 million as a result of hackers sabotaging their information systems. We have a simple, inexpensive process that will ensure your company doesn't become the next one.*

## Step Five: Determine Your Wrap-Up.

This is your call to action at the end of the presentation. You can throw in an extra piece of evidence, such as a story or a nice statistic, but you need to remember that communication is about connection and persuasion. You've just sold your listeners on something – be it an idea, a product, or a service. As you wrap up, you need to implore the audience to put your idea into action.

The wrap might sound something like this:

*We've talked about all the reasons why this software will help you save money. I'd now like to schedule a demonstration next week.*

As they say in sales, "If you don't ask, you don't get." Ask for the order. End with a call to action.

## Assembling Your Presentation Using the Formula

Now that you have all the pieces, you need to put together your presentation. A good presentation needs to follow Cicero's old rule that you should "Tell 'em what you're going to tell 'em. Tell 'em. And then tell 'em what you told 'em."

So we break our presentation into three parts. First is the preview, in which you state your Hook, your MO, and then preview your three main points. Then comes the body of the presentation, in which you go into detail, providing evidence to support each of your three points. Then there is a Recap, in which you restate your MO and three points, and then you wind up with a Wrap.

## Your Speechworks Presentation Form

(Photocopy and distribute only to people whom you'd like to have well-organized presentations.)

### Preview (Tell 'em what you're going to tell 'em)

Hook:_____

_____

Message Objective: By_____,
you will _____

Three Points

1._____
2._____
3._____

### Body of the Presentation (Tell 'em)

Point 1 _____
Evidence:_____

_____

Point 2 _____
Evidence:_____

_____

Point 3 _____

Evidence:_____

_____

## Recap and Wrap (Tell 'em what you told 'em)

Message Objective: By _____,

you will _____

Three Points

1._____

2._____

3._____

Wrap:_____

_____

_____

## The Speechworks Formula in Action

After making millions when his high-tech company's stock went public, Internet Security Systems founder Chris Klaus went on the rubber chicken circuit, telling the story of himself and his company. Talk about a challenge. Try explaining a complex business like Internet Security Systems to a bunch of Rotarians. (Most of those people are not exactly from the Internet generation).

But that's what Klaus did. And he did it successfully. In fact, the Downtown Atlanta Rotary liked his presentation so much, they ranked it the best speech of the year. On the elevator after Klaus's speech, one Rotarian was overheard saying, "I get it. I'm going to buy that stock."

### How Klaus Did It

### Klaus's Preview
**The Hook:**
Picture this:
Imagine a world where every door is wide open.
Imagine criminals can steal all your valuables without a trace.
Imagine that they are doing it in every industry.
That world exists today. It's the Internet.

**The Message Objective:**
Internet Security Systems is the leader in network security management. Understanding ISS will help you protect your sensitive information, your e-commerce transactions, and ultimately your business.

**A preview of Klaus's three points:**
Today let's take a look at three things:
The current state of Internet security.
The Internet Security Systems solution and how it began.
The future of network security: Where is this "security thing" going?

### The Body of Klaus's Presentation
**Point 1.** The current state of Internet security.
**Evidence:** Every organization in the world is now getting into the Internet. Administrators have very little knowledge of security issues. Problems with security come from hackers, disgruntled employees, criminals, and the lack of uniform international laws and regulations. Let's look at them individually.
- At a so-called "Hackers Conference" in Las Vegas recently, participants shared break-in techniques.
- Internationally, many copyright laws don't apply. We worked with a company in Japan whose system had been attacked by a company in Korea. No laws applied. So the Japanese company had to protect itself.

**Point 2.** The Internet Security Systems solution and how it began.
**Evidence:** The ISS story.

- First in my high school to be on the Internet. Klaus told a series of funny, personal stories about computer involvement.
- In 1991, I worked on a security project. The concept of the project came from the science fiction novel *Neuromancer*, the first book to use the term "cyberspace."
- We created a vulnerability scanner, to protect systems on the network. That was the beginning. The scanner worked like a guard walking around your network, looking for open windows and doors. And it worked!
- Today we work with top accounting firms to allow them to use this program and programs like it to verify the security of their big clients.

**Point 3.** So what's the future? What's hot in adaptive security management?
**Evidence:** Our management tools provide a self-curing network. You will be able to verify against your policing and adapt automatically. Like the immune system does for disease, we provide an immune system for computer networks. The problems are always changing: Last week, a major issue identified was e-mail clients having to address the problem of people sending hostile "programs" that crash their computer systems.

### Klaus's Recap and Wrap
**Recap:** So that's Internet Security Systems and the future of network security management. We've talked about:

> The current state of Internet security.
> The Internet Security Systems solution.
> The future of network security. Now you know where this "security thing" is going.

**Wrap-Up:** The last eight years have been very exciting. A new business, an IPO, travels all over the country and the world, and a growing company. Personally, I'm looking forward to next month. Today, I can afford to buy a car and next month in September, I'll turn 25. At that time, I'll be eligible to rent one.

## Coach's Commentary on the Chris Klaus Speech

Chris Klaus's presentation was a classic example of how to use the Speechworks Formula to simplify the explanation of a complex idea.

Think about all the complex information that Klaus could have laid on his listeners. He had spent years developing his product. Many entrepreneurs and high-tech experts (a.k.a. "geeks"), when asked about their product, insist on boring listeners with all the details of how the product was developed.

Not Klaus. He focused on what the Rotarians needed to know. As businesspersons, they needed to know the state of Internet security, the general ideas behind how ISS has solved the problem, and the future of the Internet security problem. The Rotarians also wanted to know about ISS as a potential investment. And that's what Klaus focused on. He focused on what was in it for his listeners.

And notice how Klaus handled the complexity of his product – he didn't try to explain the technology in too much detail. Rather, he used analogies to illustrate how the system worked.

## The Formula: It's Not Just for Presentations

*Excerpt from a Socratic dialogue overheard at Speechworks.*

*Grasshopper\*:* Master, I love the Formula. But I need more than a process for putting together formal presentations. I need something that will help me when I go in to see Dev.

*Master:* Who is Dev, Grasshopper?

*Grasshopper:* Dev is the southeastern regional division supervisor with supervisory responsibility over the local operations section of the distribution manufacturing business unit.

*Master:* Your boss?

---

\* For those non-geeks who may have picked up a copy of this book, Grasshopper was the name of the student in the old *Kung Fu* television series. Grasshopper was always learning at the heel of his learned Master. "Snatch the pebble from my hand, Grasshopper, and you will learn the ways of speed and wisdom." Also, Grasshopper is pronounced "Grasshoppaaaahhhhhh."

*Grasshopper:* Yes, Master. My boss. He scares me.

*Master:* Grasshopper, you can use the Formula when you speak to Dev.

*Grasshopper:* Really, Master? Please tell me how. I want to learn the ways of the Formula.

*Master:* The Formula's principles apply to all sorts of presentations, even one-on-one presentations to your boss, the man you know as Dev. Let me tell you a story, Grasshopper. When I was practicing law, I, too, had to report to a boss, a man not unlike your Dev. My boss was quite a lawyer, a man of legendary stature at the firm. He only dealt with the presidents and CEOs of our firm's clients. I never dealt with such exalted people. I only worked with the middle-level managers and their problems. Needless to say, my boss was a little intimidating for a utility geek like myself. His name, of course, was not Dev. It was Vic [name changed to protect the author's neck]. Vic would occasionally call me into his office so I could report on the progress of a

## WHY DO WE GEEKS SPEAK THIS WAY?

If we geeks are so smart, why can't we speak English? Well, let's just say that we've been in our cubicles a very long time, says Bob Jannarone, a psychology Ph.D., who also founded the Atlanta software firm Netuitive. "When you spend so much time building the drill, it's easy to forget about the hole."

In other words, those of us who know a lot about a subject tend to be people who have a deep understanding of the details of a process, but can lose sight of that process's greater significance.

So tax geeks know the details of a tax code, but may have a hard time telling you how it impacts you. Computer geeks know how to program a computer, but they have a hard time telling you what the program does in layman's terms. Economist geeks run incredibly complex economic forecasting models, but they can't explain the broad significance of their conclusions.

We geeks also are lousy communicators because of our personality type. We enjoy the detailed logic of our specialty and often don't understand that others just aren't interested. "A software code is a logical sequence to solve a problem," says Bob Zack, who is president of Netuitive. "And that's the way a programmer thinks. That kind of personality thinks in terms of exquisite step-by-step logic. And when they explain what they do, they want you to know about that exquisite logic."

big case. I'd start by telling him all the details of the various arguments I was making and how the other side was responding. He'd interrupt me and say, "I ask you the time of day and you tell me how to build a [extremely bad word] watch."

**WII-FM**

*Grasshopper*: Oh, I get it, Master – you weren't telling him information he needed to know. You didn't begin by addressing what was in it for him.

*Master*: That's right, Grasshopper. What do you think Vic really needed to know?

*Grasshopper*: You said he only dealt with the presidents of the firm's clients. I suppose he just wanted the big picture so he could report to his contacts about the status of the case.

*Master*: That's right, Grasshopper. I should have said, "Vic, it looks like we will go to trial next week. We have a strong case, but so does the other side."

*Grasshopper*: And then you could have backed up those basic points with evidence.

*Master*: Excellent, Grasshopper. You are learning the way of the Formula. Vic didn't care about the details. I should have started with the big picture preview and then filled in with the back-up information, just like the Formula says.

*Grasshopper*: Gee, Master, the Formula really does apply to more than just formal business presentations. Wouldn't it be great if we all used the Formula every day?

*Master*: That is my dream, Grasshopper. That is my dream.

### How Canst Thou Use the Formula? Let Us Count the Ways.
### 1. In putting together a presentation.

No matter how long or how short your presentation, you can use the Speechworks Formula. If it's a short presentation, use three simple points, three pieces of evidence, and you're done. If you're giving a long presentation, have three general points in support of your MO with lots of subpoints.

## 2. To telescope a presentation when you're cut short.
The great thing about the Formula is that if you're scheduled for one hour and the long-winded goober who went ahead of you has left you with ten minutes before the lunch break, you can cut quickly to the chase. You've got your MO, your three points, your evidence, a hook, and a wrap. Just get through them quickly, without going into the details, and you've got a nice short presentation.

## 3. In writing a memo, letter, or a magazine article.
John Jantson, a consultant at Kurt Salmon Associates, wrote an article for a trade publication using the Formula for his organizational structure. Remember, just tell the readers the MO at the beginning and the three key points.

## 4. E-mails.
The number-one problem with e-mails is that they're usually free-form brain dumps. Use the Formula to give your e-mails a clear point.

## 5. In organizing a meeting.
Begin the meeting with your MO: "This is what we're going to accomplish at this meeting." Then follow with a three-point agenda. "We're going to cover the following three areas."

## 6. In briefing your boss.
Start with an MO: "The project is going to succeed." Then give three supporting points: "We're going to finish on time, on budget, and the work is going to be high quality."

## 7. In a job interview.
"If you hire me, I'm going to be able to reduce your warehouse costs by $500,000 a year." Offer three points: "I've done it before. I have a plan for how to do it in your company. I already know and get along with everyone on your team."

## 8. In asking your wife to play golf.
MO: "If you let me play golf, the entire household will be happier." Three points: "I'm going crazy and need a day smacking around a little white ball. When I get home I'll give the kids a bath. Tomorrow, I'll watch the kids while you play tennis."

## Keepers

1. Before any communication, think about what will be your Message Objective.
2. Limit yourself to no more than three points.
3. Always support your points with solid evidence, including stories (lots of stories), personal examples, expert testimony, analogies, killer quotes, and stats and facts.

## CHAPTER 2

*"Good communication is like a pencil:
it has to have a point."*
**– Speechworks**

# The Message Objective: The Cornerstone of Persuasive, Simple Communication

Great skills often begin with a single fundamental: a cornerstone skill.

In golf, the cornerstone skill is the fluid, repeatable swing. Golf has plenty of nuances like putting, chipping, and pitching. But once you've mastered a basic swing (no small task) you're a long way to being a good golfer.

In writing, the cornerstone skill is the simple declarative sentence. Learn to write one good sentence. From there you can string together lots of those good sentences into a good novel, a good memo, a good legal brief, or a good letter. Like golf, there are lots of other things to learn. But it all starts with learning to write one good sentence.

In spoken communication, the cornerstone skill is forming a clear Message Objective. Learn how to craft a clear MO (it's a lot easier than learning to hit a golf ball, I promise), and you're a long way toward being able to make complex things simple in a persuasive manner.

## The Components of the Message Objective

The Message Objective always brings together two things:

1. Your goal of persuading the audience to do something, and
2. What's in it for the listener.

Your Message Objective should sound something like this: By [buying into my ideas or buying my product], you will [achieve your goals].

By crossing your goal with the interest of your listeners, your message will be on target.

So, for example:

- **To the chief information officer:** By purchasing the QR545 computer, you will improve your office efficiency and save your employees hours of work.
- **To the head of a division:** By committing resources to upgrade the Internet scanner's report outputs, you will make our clients happier with the product and sell more Internet scanners.
- **To a group of lawyers:** By understanding the fundamentals of the real estate appraisal process, you will be better able to serve your clients.
- **To a lawyer's client:** By understanding what types of documents are considered trade secret, you will avoid inadvertently disclosing those documents to the public and compromising the company's most important proprietary information.

## The First Thing the MO Gives You: Clarity

How many times have you been in a presentation and you didn't understand the presenter's overall purpose?

There's Susan. She's up at the whiteboard. She's drawing pictures. But what she's saying sounds suspiciously like a stream-of-consciousness brain dump.

That never happens if you begin with a Message Objective. By stating a Message Objective right at the beginning of your presentation, you will always have a focused presentation. So few presentations have a clear purpose and clear listener benefit. But the MO gives you that from the start.

### The Second Thing the MO Gives You: Your Listener's Undivided Attention

Understanding what's in it for the listener is the key to keeping a listener's interest. Think about what happens when you declare that the listener will get something by listening to you. It's a challenge to them. You're throwing down the gauntlet. "If you buy into this new way of programming these computers, your company is going to get filthy stinkin' rich." Of course, maybe the listener doesn't buy it immediately. He may cross his arms, thrust out his chin, and say, "Oh yeah? Prove it." But now you definitely have his attention, and there is no doubt in his mind what you're up to. Gone are the days of meandering brain dumps and incomprehensible scribbles on the whiteboard.

### The Third Thing the MO Gives You: Simplification of Complexity

By forcing you to focus on the listener's interests, you will magically remove 91 percent of the complexity from your communication. That's because of the three Speechworks Principles of Listening to Complex Subject Matter.

**Principle 1:** Most people want to know how technology (or any other complex subject) will make them richer, thinner, happier, or have better sex.

**Principle 2.** If someone wants to know how the new tax law works, chances are that they will give you some indication of interest. An "indication of interest" would be a statement like "Tell me exactly how the new tax law works, Jim. I'm interested in details."

**Principle 3.** Absent an "indication of interest" (see principle 2), you should avoid explaining the details of your e-mail platform to your listener. Rather,

A major key to speaking with clarity about complex things is simply to realize that most of the time the listener isn't interested in the complexity. Rather, she wants to know how that complex stuff affects her. Put another way, all people wear imaginary headsets tuned to their favorite radio station, WII-FM, which stands for "What's in It for Me?" The best communicators focus only on what is in it for the listeners.

limit discussions or explanations of your area of expertise to those areas described in the first principle.

### A New Game Show Coming This Fall: *Who Wants to Be Understood?*

*(Winners of this game don't need to go on to* Who Wants to Be a Millionaire? *because they usually become millionaires anyway.)*

Now let's play the new game show that's been riveting business audiences everywhere, *Who Wants to Be Understood?* Our game-show contestants are real people who have learned how to master the art of explaining complex things.

### First Contestant: Jim Verlander

**The situation:** Our first contestant is Jim Verlander. Jim is a software engineer for Webtone, a company that provides customer service software to on-line banking systems. Jim was planning a presentation to the president of a bank. He wanted to persuade the bank president of the value of his company's new e-mail response software. His plan was to begin with a detailed explanation of the inner workings of his gee-whiz technology, complete with an explanation of how the software enabled the bank to automatically respond to thousands of e-mail messages from the bank's on-line customers.

**The problem:** Bank presidents don't care about software. They care about money. What a surprise! They want to get rich. Or should we say rich-ER.

**WII-FM:** So how do we recast Jim's presentation to focus on the WII-FM of the bank president? Jim came up with a great presentation that focused primarily on how the software had helped other banks get happier on-line customers and make more money. He included some details about the capabilities of the software, but only in the context of how those capabilities served the primary goal of making customers happy. He explained how the software could respond to thousands of e-mails per day, helping reduce the numbers of persons needed to staff the bank's call response center.

## Second contestant: Stan Yarbrough

**The situation:** Our next contestant is Stan Yarbrough. Stan is a consultant with the North Highland Company, a high-tech consulting firm. His background is in telecommunications. He wanted to convince a business owner to abandon the "private network" that connected the company's worldwide system of computers in favor of a "virtual private network." His original presentation was highly technical, explaining in detail all the reasons why the new technology was superior.

**The problem:** Most business owners couldn't care less about the details of how computer networks operate. They only care about how this new system will help his company become more successful.

**WII-FM:** So how did we recast Stan's presentation? We focused on the owner's primary interests. We talked about how the new system would save the company money. He also described how the new system would be more secure than the existing system. Finally, we made sure that we discussed how this new system would make the company more competitive in the marketplace.

## Confessions of a Budget Geek: A Fable

I was a budget geek.

When I was a newspaper reporter (that was before I was a lawyer/utility geek), I sometimes covered county government in Westchester County, New York. Part of my job included an annual budget analysis where I had to take the complexity of a $1 billion government budget and boil it down to a few key points for the newspaper's readers. This was no small task; the budget document weighed five pounds and measured three inches thick. The jail portion of the budget had been slashed and the utility portion had been padded. The cuts to the welfare budget were interesting because of all the political infighting involved.

How did we sift through it all to write a story no longer than 16 column inches? We focused first on the primary thing that the readers needed and wanted to know, and suddenly it all became clear: How is this budget going to impact the reader's pocketbooks? In other words, how does the budget impact taxes?

### MORAL: LISTENER FOCUS UNRAVELS COMPLEXITY

The same process that we used in cutting through the complexity of the county budget is the same process any geek worth his Hewlett-Packard scientific calculator must use in cutting through the complexity of his ideas. Begin by focusing on what is in it for your listeners.

### How to Become a Winner on *Who Wants to Be Understood?*: Just a Little Thought Before Speaking

Usually, just a little thought will tell you what your listener is really interested in. For example, you know that your secretary probably doesn't care about the details of your new software creation. You know a prospective client cares first about how the software will help him make or save money. The key is just to get in the habit of considering what your listeners care about.

### Play the Home Version

Here's a little exercise. Say you're a tax accountant at a top accounting firm and you read in your industry newsletter that Congress has just decided to adjust the way that it taxes corporations. Of course, since you are a true accounting geek, this event ranks up there on the excitement scale with a weekend-long *X-Files* marathon on FX. Squirming with glee, you look up the law on the Internet and print it out.

Great news! The law is extremely detailed!

You spend two days working through it and trying to figure out how it works. Your time spent sifting through the new law gives you a feeling of exhilaration that is almost erotic in nature. You've finally figured it out.

Now, here is the game. You emerge from your office and no matter who you run into next, you are going to tell them about the new tax law. But the game here is that you have to adjust what you say based on who you run into.

What do you say if you run into . . .

**Your boss?** A major rainmaker at the firm, he cares little about the details of accounting, but speaks daily with the CEO of your firm's biggest client.
Write Your Answer Here:

_____

_____

_____

_____

**Your business partner?** A fellow tax geek, he gets even more excited than you do about changes in the tax laws.
Write Your Answer Here:

_____

_____

_____

_____

**Your client?** She's the chief financial officer of a major corporation.
Write Your Answer Here:

_____

_____

_____

_____

**Your neighbor?** He's made a lot of money with a business that does pool maintenance.
Write Your Answer Here:

_____

_____

_____

_____

**Your secretary?** She complains every time you put anything on her desk.
Write Your Answer Here:

_____

_____

_____

_____

**Your wife?** She loves you in spite of your unusual enthusiasm for mechanical pencils.
Write Your Answer Here:

_____

_____

_____

_____

### Answer Key:
### Compare Your Answers to the Following Suggested Answers

**Your boss:** Since he's a rainmaker, he probably doesn't care about the technicalities that you enjoy so much. But he probably would like to know something to tell his client. How about, "I just finished reading a new tax law that will have major impact on your client. You might want to let them know that this law could cause a significant increase in their tax bill if they aren't careful. I'll be happy to meet with their accounting department to discuss it." He may then give you an indication that he wants to know more detail to tell his client. Follow his lead to determine how much detail.

**Your business partner:** Since he's a fellow tax geek, he probably wants the joy of reading it himself. Or maybe he's read it already. Try, "What did you think of the change in the corporate tax?" But again, even a fellow geek in this situation probably doesn't want a brain dump on the details of the tax law.

**Your client:** What you say to your client depends in part on whether you're speaking to the client's tax department or the CEO. If it's the CEO, you want to alert her that there is a new law that could affect her business's bottom line. Try,

"Sue, I just read a new tax law that could raise your taxes by 10 percent next quarter if you don't make a few adjustments to the way you account for corporate travel. I'll talk to your accounting department ASAP to discuss it."

If your contact is not the CEO but is with your client's tax department, then you probably need to say something like, "Did you see the new tax law? We need to discuss some changes that you guys may need to make in your accounting software. If you don't change the way you account for corporate travel, you could see an increase in your taxes by 10 percent next quarter."

**Your neighbor:** Of course you have no business relationship with your neighbor, but you want to be helpful to him. Maybe he'll decide to use you for his accounting someday. How about, "Bob, you better check with your accountant on this new tax law. It looks like you may have to make some adjustments in how you account for corporate travel. We're telling all our clients about it."

**Your secretary:** Her interest in the tax law is the amount of work it means for her. How about "Well, Jane, it looks like we're going to be busy for the next few months working with our clients on this new tax law."

**Your wife:** Your wife's main interest is the security of your job and whether you'll make more money as a result of the new tax law. "Judy, Congress just passed another Full Employment Act for Accountants. This new tax law is going to mean lots of work for me for the next two years."

## Keepers
1. A clear MO will ensure that everyone knows what you're trying to accomplish.
2. Telling a listener what's in it for them challenges them to pay attention. Keep in mind that your listener's favorite radio station is WII-FM.
3. Focusing on the listener's interests will ensure that your message is no more complex than necessary.

## CHAPTER 3

*"The secret to being a bore . . .*
*tell everything."*
– **Voltaire**

# Dozens of Reasons to Limit Your Presentation to No More Than Three Points

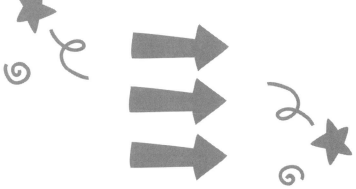

In the Speechworks Clear Communications Code, Section 14, Paragraph 6, there is the following provision.

*"Presentations shall have no more than THREE points given in support of a presentation's Message Objective. There shall not be four points. Nor shall there be five. Six is definitely out. As are seven, eight, and nine. Ten points? Fuggeddaboudit! While there may be two points or one point, never shall there be more than three points."*

## Why No More Than Three Points?

People can't remember more than three points.

Three points have impact.

Boiling down to three points ensures that you focus on the major benefits to the listener, rather than delving into a level of technical detail that is not needed or wanted.

## Take It from a Lobbyist Who Focuses on Complex Utility Issues

I have a friend who lobbies politicians on behalf of a large gas utility. The kinds of issues he talks to them about are as complex as they come. For example, try explaining to politicians with no regulatory accounting background why they should support a plan to change the way a gas utility does its accounting. Here's what my friend said is his secret: "What I do is limit my appeals to three major points."

For example, he might say that the new accounting is needed for three reasons:

1. It's good for the rate-payers (that's what the politicians care most about). And then he goes into the level of detail necessary to show how the rates will go down as a result of the accounting change.
2. It's good for the utility (the politicians want a healthy utility). And then he explains with the level of detail necessary to show how the new system will ensure a healthy balance sheet for the utility.
3. It's good for the state (the politicians want a healthy state). Finally, he will go into the level of detail necessary to show that the accounting system will be good for the state's economy by keeping down rates and attracting industry to the area.

## Or Take it from Bill Nye, the Science Guy

Bill Nye, the Science Guy produces a popular national program on public television in which he explains the complexities of science to children. And what's his secret?

"The key to explaining things on my show," Nye told me, "has been to distill the ideas to get to the fundamental notions and to exclude the other interesting but not-so-focused information. . . . On the dinosaur show, we make *two points*. These are called "learning objectives" in the education industry. A learning objective is something you can test the viewer, reader, listener, or student on."

So on the dinosaur show, his two points were:

- We know that dinosaurs once lived because we find their fossil bones.
- Dinosaurs and humans did not live at the same time.

In other words, if you want to make complex things simple, take the lead from Bill Nye, the Science Guy. Pick your "learning objectives" and make sure that your listeners get those points.

## "But I Have More Than Three Points"

"I *have* to have six points! I can't get it down to three."

We hear that in our workshops regularly. In that case, you have two choices. You can boil it down to three points – or you can find yourself in violation of the Speechworks Clear Communications Code. The penalty for violating that code is imposed on your listeners through your boring, unfocused presentations.

If you choose to comply with the code, then here is what you do. You put down all your ideas onto a sheet of paper. And then you group them into three buckets.

Let me give you an example of how it works.

## Wally White, Real Estate Appraiser

Wally White, managing director of the Atlanta appraisal group for Cushman & Wakefield, spoke to a law firm about real estate appraising. Obviously, there were more than three points he could make. There are a half-dozen different levels of appraiser certification. Each of these types of appraisers can be used for different types of appraisals. And then there are the different types of reports that appraisers issue. Not only that, but the law firm had made a special request that White talk about the complexities of property valuation.

How could he get all that into three points?

Easy! He just put all the information into three buckets. Here's what White said:

What you need to know to help your clients breaks down into the three Rs of real estate appraising.

The **Requirements** for becoming an appraiser. This section would be a summary of the different types of appraisers and their certification requirements.

The **Reliability** of the different appraisers in a variety of circumstances. This section would explain how each type of appraiser is considered reliable in different circumstances.

The **Reports** issued by appraisers. This section would detail the important contents of the reports. Wally also included a summary of how the property valuations were included in the reports.

### Kevin Overcash, Computer Programmer

Or consider a presentation given by Kevin Overcash to his superiors at Internet Security Systems. Kevin is a career programmer. He admits that he is just now getting comfortable with being known as a "computer geek." It's become cool to be a geek, he says, and the younger programmers even call themselves "geeks." But accepting the label is still a little hard for Kevin. "There's thirty years of being called that in a derogatory sense," he says. "So it's still somewhat difficult to get over that history."

Kevin had been trying for some time to get his superiors to change the way that one of his company's products, "Internet Scanner," an Internet security product, issues printed reports on activity monitored by the program. Overcash's pleas, he suspects, merely came across as complaining. But while attending a Speechworks workshop, he decided to try once again. He put together a presentation aimed at a superior who happened to be in the workshop with him that week. Rather than touting numerous technical reasons for the change, Overcash tightened his presentation as follows.

His **Message Objective:** Improving the reports on Internet Scanner will help us sell more Internet Scanners.

His strategy was to develop three points focused on what he knew were hot buttons for his superior:
- People who are interested in security products are interested in professionalism. The reports from Internet

Scanner make his firm look unprofessional.
- The reports actually create more work and frustration for our users.
- Our clients often give the reports in Internet Scanner to their superiors. If the reports don't look professional, it makes our clients look bad to their bosses.

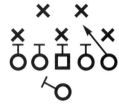

Overcash's presentation worked; he sold his superiors on the idea of committing resources to improve the quality of the reports.

Why did he make the sale? He had a strategy, a plan.

"I really focused on points that I knew would touch a nerve, rather than me just going in and complaining," he said. In other words, he tightened up his presentation to the hot buttons. Less really is more.

## Putting the Three Points in Order: There's No Simple Answer

We're going to throw you a loop here. There is no simple answer as to how to order your three points—only theories.

Some say that your best point should be either first or last. "Research shows that jurors remember best what I said first and last," commented University of Georgia law professor Ron Carlson in a *USA Today* article. Carlson's point illustrates the psychological principles of "primacy" and "recency," which hold that with long lists of things, people tend to remember those things that come first or last on the list. But with only three points, this issue is less important. However, certainly you should position the most important point either first or last.

## Here's a Novel Idea: Use Your Best Judgment!

As much as I'd like to offer you that simple answer on how to order your points, I cannot. The fact of the matter is that how you order your points comes down to your judgment. (Gasp!!!)

Assess what you think will appeal most to this particular listener and decide whether you think that you should begin or end with the most important point. Say you're pitching a new technology to different departments within a prospect company. If you're pitching the president of the company, you may decide to lead with how your technology will make the company more competitive in the marketplace. But if you're pitching the chief financial officer, you're going to probably want to lead with how your technology is inexpensive or offers a great value financially.

Ultimately, what matters most is that you simply go through the thought process of considering what is most important to this particular listener or group of listeners and then shaping your presentation accordingly.

### Some Tried-and-True Narrative Forms for Your Three-Point Presentations

Often you don't want to organize a presentation around three reasons that the MO is true. Sometimes a narrative form is more appropriate. Here are three we like:

- Past, Present, and Future
- Advantages, Disadvantages, Call to Action
- Situation, Crisis, Solution

### Past, Present, and Future

We worked with a food franchise executive who was planning a presentation designed to revitalize sagging relationships with mall owners. It seems that the franchisees had not been maintaining clean outlets in the food courts. At first blush, you might think that the most important point to make to the mall owners is that "we've changed and here's how." But the executive wanted to work with a more narrative style, describing what had happened in the past, what they were doing about it now, and how that would benefit the mall owners in the future. Here is what she said:

**MO:** By revitalizing our relationship, you will be positioning your food courts for maximum profits in the future.

**The past:** We realize that there have been problems and we realize what the causes were.

**The present:** We are doing the following to correct those past problems.

**The future:** As a result of these corrections, you should see increased profits and traffic in your food courts.

This was a nice narrative format that focused on the listeners' interests. But notice that the crucial point to be made – "we've changed and here's how" – actually appeared as the second point in her presentation, instead of the first or third spot we'd discussed earlier. So use your judgment. A good narrative format based on your assessment of listener interests should give you a sense of how to order your points.

## Advantages, Disadvantages, Call to Action

We worked with a union negotiator for a major lumber company as he planned a presentation urging some mill workers to vote down a union.

**MO:** A vote against the union is a vote for security and a happier workplace.

1. Advantages of the status quo
2. Disadvantages of being unionized
3. Vote "no" for the union

This is a simple but very effective narrative format that works because it's a variation on the way many people make hard decisions. Many of us make a line down the middle of a page and we write all the advantages of taking action on one side and the disadvantages on the other. You then make your decision based on which column has the longer list. Listeners can relate easily to this thought process.

## Situation, Crisis, Solution

Sometimes you're trying to explain how your idea or business proposal solves a particular problem. A classic three-point organizational format for such a presentation is "situation, crisis, solution."

**MO:** By buying into my idea, this company will solve a problem that will save it millions of dollars.

- Situation: The situation is [insert brief description of situation].
- Crisis: If the problem isn't resolved, we will reach a crisis: we will have to spend untold thousands of dollars.
- Solution: The solution is [insert the proposed solution].

Here's an example. Say you've invented a new Internet program for handling thousands of e-mails and you want to sell your company on using this new platform to interact with customers over the Internet.

**MO:** By going with the XYZ e-mail system, we will be positioning this company for long-term satisfaction of a new breed of customer.

**Situation:** Our new breed of customer expects to interact with us over the Internet via e-mail.

**Crisis:** As the number of this new breed of customer grows, we will be unable to handle this growth if we remain with our current e-mail platform.

**Solution:** The new e-mail platform that I propose today will position the company to handle all of our e-mail needs now and for many years to come, thereby resulting in satisfaction of our new breed of customer.

### Situation, Crisis, Solution for a One-on-One Sales Presentation

In one-on-one sales presentations, it's sometimes inappropriate to give a formal pitch. One on one, you usually want to have more of a conversation. Here's a three-point pitch that works great.

**MO:** By meeting today, we're going to find out whether we can find a solution to your data processing problems.

**Situation:** Ask the prospect lots of questions designed to understand the data processing situation they have now.

**Crisis:** Discuss how their current data processing solutions are working. The key here is to lead the prospect into complaining about the current system. You want to find the problems. Where is the pain? Otherwise, you probably won't be able to make a sale.

**Solution:** Having heard the current situation and problems, you need to provide a solution, presumably the one provided by your company. You then need to show how your data processing system solves all of their problems.

### Convincing a Friend to See a Movie

I include this section for my own self-preservation. I have a relative, let's call him Charlie. Charlie is big movie fan, but is also something of a geek. How big a geek? Well, let's just say Charlie has a subscription to the magazine *Physics Today*.

Now, I am close to Charlie and like him a lot. But I dread his movie recommendations. He seems to think that reporting on a movie means that you must recount the entire plot, including all subplots and choice snippets of dialogue. Such a tendency is, of course, very geeky.

Charlie doesn't seem to understand that the communication process should be founded primarily on understanding the interest of the listener. Remember, Charlie, all I really care about is whether it's a movie that I will like. So, if you're reading, Charlie, for all future movie recommendations, please limit your remarks to the following format.

**MO:** *The Blair Witch Project* was lots of fun and extremely scary. You'll love it.

➡ **Point 1:** It's filmed like a documentary with handheld cameras to simulate three friends going camping to investigate the legend of the Blair Witch.

➡ **Point 2:** The acting is terrific. The film really feels like a home movie about three young people on a camping trip gone bad.

➡ **Point 3:** It scared the hell out of me even though there were no special effects.

Okay, Charlie. That's it. I don't need to know any more than that!

## Keepers

1. Limiting your points to three adds power and memorability to your presentation.
2. Boil your points down to three by putting them into three buckets.
3. Experiment with different narrative formats for your three-point presentations.

*"High tech ... High touch."*
**– John Naisbitt, *Megatrends***

# Make It Sing with Evidence: How to Make Your Presentation Exciting

In our workshops, we repeatedly hear people ask how they can make their dull presentations more exciting. "I only talk about financials," said a financial analyst from Coca-Cola. "How do I make that exciting?"

It can be done, my friends. It's all in the evidence. If your evidence is exciting, then you're going to have an interesting speech.

### What Is Evidence?

By evidence, what do we mean? Think S.P.E.A.K.S.: Stories, Personal experiences, Expert testimony, Analogies, Kwotes, and Statistics (as in numbers and facts). Your evidence, and the quality of your evidence, will:

• Separate you from the other presenters.
• Make your case.
• Make your presentation memorable.

### Stories: The Keys to the Kingdom of Exciting Presentations

In the Speechworks Clear Communications Code, Section 12, Paragraph 8, is the following provision.

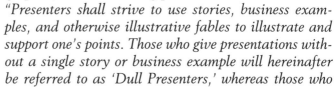

*"Presenters shall strive to use stories, business examples, and otherwise illustrative fables to illustrate and support one's points. Those who give presentations without a single story or business example will hereinafter be referred to as 'Dull Presenters,' whereas those who succeed in including stories in their presentations shall be referred to as 'Exciting Presenters' and shall be deemed worthy of rising to great heights in their respective trades."*

Stories comprise the most memorable type of evidence available to the communicator and speaker. A salesman for a major shipping company wanted to win the logistics business of a new dot-com that sold sporting equipment. He wanted to make the point that good e-tailers have more than just a good Web site. Good e-tailers also have finely tuned fulfillment processes that get the products to the customer on time with no surprises.

To make his point, he told the story of how he ordered from a major Internet toy e-tailer a Big Wheel racer for his daughter. He then recounted a parade of horrible experiences in which the racer showed up too late for Christmas and in the wrong color. The story had impact and made his presentation interesting and exciting.

Think of how much less powerful it would have been had he simply made the bland statement that "You are going to need a strong fulfillment process to keep your customers happy." Without the story, his presentation would have been dull.

## Every Business Has Its Stories: Use Them

Every business has an arsenal of stories that illustrate the power of that company's products and ideas. Use them to illustrate your presentations.

Consider Optio Software, which has software designed to reduce the cost of buying preprinted forms for hospitals. When presenting the product to prospective buyers, Optio doesn't just describe the software. Instead, the Optio sales force tells the story of Saint Francis Medical Center, a 264-bed hospital in Cape Girardeau, Missouri. Before working with Optio, the hospital had to buy preprinted forms for everything from employee pay stubs to lab test results. But with Optio's MedForms software, the hospital was able to print those forms on any laser printer, eliminating the costs of buying preprinted forms. In two years, the hospital stopped buying 116 different forms, saving over $1 million.

That is a wonderful, detailed, persuasive story.

Bob Peterson, vice president of Health Care Solutions for Optio, fully understands that, when talking about complex products like MedForms, sales people must describe the product in terms of the results that buyers can expect. "I want my people to be professional storytellers," Peterson says.

## What Makes a Good Story?

The best stories do three things. They are:

• **Detailed.** Notice that Optio doesn't talk about an anonymous "large Midwestern hospital." It describes Saint Francis Medical Center, a 264-bed hospital in Cape Girardeau, Missouri. Detail persuades the listener by helping him actually see the story unfolding before his eyes.

• **Relevant to the listener's situation.** If you're giving a sales presentation, you want your listeners to be able to put themselves in the shoes of your story's protagonist. That shipping company salesman wouldn't tell the story about the Big Wheel racer to a company that wasn't an Internet e-tailer.

• **Short.** The best stories make the point quickly. Too often, we see presenters who fancy themselves old-fashioned raconteurs. Their stories go on forever and only get to the point after much patience on the part of the listener. Set it up fast and then make your point. Don't drag it out.

### Expose Yourself: Use Personal Examples

Weaving yourself into a presentation is a wonderful way to help build relationships between yourself and your listeners. When people know a little about you, they tend to like you more than they would otherwise.

I always work into my presentations my background as a newspaper reporter and a lawyer. We worked recently with Stan Gay, who played football for the University of Alabama and the Atlanta Falcons. Now he sells protective surgical gowns for Kimberly-Clark Corporation. We suggested that he weave into his presentation something about his athletic background. He immediately suggested that he could emphasize to his prospects how, as a former football player, he understands the importance of protective clothing. Great stuff!

### And Don't Underestimate the Power of Personal Connection

We worked with a money management firm, INVESCO, in helping them pitch for a large piece of business up in the New York area. The presenter mentioned at some point that he went to Fordham University. It turned out that one of the key decision-makers in the room that day had gone to Fordham.

Guess who got the business?

They didn't win only because of the Fordham connection. But the connection helped tighten the relationship that eventually led to winning the business.

### Expert Testimony

If your listener doesn't believe you, maybe they'll believe an expert. These days, it seems that you can't attend a presentation on e-business and Internet commerce without someone citing a study by a consulting firm known as the Gartner Group.

Recently, we worked with Netuitive, a start-up that provides software to Internet companies. The software enables the companies to project fluctuations in activity on their Web site, thereby allowing them to avoid performance problems created by spikes in Web site activity.

Their presentation included a quote from, who else, Gartner Group: "Action item: Invest in applications management to proactively identify key indicators that signal potential availability and performance problems before they impact users."

## Analogies:
## They Can Drive Home Your Point Like a Hammer

Analogies are wonderful shortcuts when trying to explain complex ideas or processes. But for some reason, presenters often don't use those analogies. I encourage you to use them. They can be extremely persuasive.

Consider an analogy created by Walter West, director of business development for MEAG Power, which sells power in Georgia. He wanted to come up with an easy way to make people understand how power buyers could now buy power in bulk, in advance, at a low price. In reality, the product involved complex power purchase agreements. But he wanted to explain it simply. Here's what he came up with.

*Electricity is one of the only products you cannot store. Unlike buying pencils, which you can store in a warehouse, you buy electricity at the moment you need it at the prevailing price at that moment. Wouldn't it be nice if you could buy power like you buy pencils? Wouldn't it be nice if you could go to Sam's Club when you see a special advertised price, so that you could stock up? In a sense, West explained, that is what MEAG can now allow its customers to do. MEAG's new product, in a sense, allows you to buy power in bulk at a low price and store it at that low price until you use it.*

## Coming Up with Analogies:
## First Check to See If You're Already Using Analogies for the Product

Much of the time, you will find that your business uses analogies all the time without a second thought. The key is to just be aware of them and use them.

When working with Netuitive, we suggested using an analogy to explain their complex software. Bob Zack, their president, said, "Well, we always say that running an e-commerce site is currently a lot like being in a souped-up Ferrari. But imagine it's a Ferrari with all sorts of gauges that project where you will be in five hours, but also has a blacked-out windshield preventing the driver from seeing where he will be in the next two minutes. In other words, Web sites do well predicting long-term trends in usage, but have no way of knowing whether they're about to get blindsided by a Mack truck crossing an intersection a quarter-mile away."

With that analogy, I immediately understood why it was important to have a program like Netuitive's that can predict short-term fluctuations in Web site usage. Zack put the analogy in his presentation.

Check to see if you're already using some analogies and plug them in.

## The Speechworks Analogy-Generation Machine

Here's an analogy-creation technique that works.

Gather two or three coworkers for a twenty-minute brainstorming session.

1. Write down the name of your product. For example, "Time Management Software."
2. Write down five commonplace items or services. For example,
   • Telephone
   • Bike messenger service
   • Swimming pool
   • Steak knives
   • Stretch limousine
3. Come up with five ways in which your product is like each of the listed items. For example, Time Management Software is like a . . .
   • Telephone, because even if you ignore it, it will interrupt you with a loud ring and get you on track.
   • Bike messenger service, because it will ensure that you deliver your products on time.
   • Swimming pool, because it keeps you cool and relaxed

when the heat in your office gets unbearable.

- Set of steak knives, because it allows you to cut through the gristle of your day.
- Stretch limousine, because it gets you to your destination on time and in style.

If you work hard at coming up with analogies for each item, you will end up with a couple you like. Don't worry if you're analogy isn't perfect. Remember, you're just trying to get your idea across in a way that connects with the listener.

## Killer Quotes

Sometimes a quote says what you want in just the right way. If so, then use it as evidence to support your points. Here are a few that we like:

> *"We owe a lot to Thomas Edison – if it wasn't for him, we'd all be watching television by candlelight."* – Milton Berle.

> *"Be sincere, be brief, be seated."* – FDR, on the secret to a good speech.

> *"The problem with the rat race is that even if you win, you're still a rat."* – Lily Tomlin.

## Statistics: Make 'Em Sing

Many years ago, I took a statistics course at the local community college. My professor had such a heavy French accent that I could only understand about a third of the words he said. I learned everything instead from reading the textbook. Most presenters who use a lot of statistics don't fare much better than my professor. Statistics are the most commonly used yet least persuasive form of evidence. But there are some keys to using numbers effectively.

If you have a lot of statistics or financial information, don't go over every number during the presentation. Focus on one or two key numbers, and then hand out the rest and take questions.

## Let Us See the Statistics in Unique Ways

If you're trying to show how the cost of computing has declined, give us something that will be memorable. Say you're talking about the drop in the cost of computers over the last twenty-five years. Rather than give the actual percentage decline, you might do a comparison to bring the figure to life. You might say that if the cost of cars had declined by the same degree, a Jaguar would cost only $50.

An acre is 43,560 square feet. To help your audience see an acre, tell them to visualize a football field without the end zones.

In a discussion of inflation, don't throw a bunch of meaningless percentages at me. Tell me what a loaf of bread cost 20 years ago as compared with today.

## Tell Me the Story behind the Numbers

Don't just tell me sales are down. Dig behind the numbers to show me an example of why sales are down. You might start by showing how sales dropped 5 percent last month because of poor weather. Well, how does poor weather cause reduced sales? Maybe you can tell me a story about a single salesman and his inability to make his rounds due to the excessive rain.

## Keepers

1. The key to making your presentation interesting is the quality of your evidence.
2. Detailed, relevant stories make the most persuasive evidence.
3. In addition to stories, use personal examples, expert testimony, analogies, killer quotes, and interesting statistics and facts.

## CHAPTER 5

*"Trust your gut."*
– **Barbara Walters**

# The Hook: How to Make a First Impression with Impact

With the hook, you grab your listeners by the lapels and force them to pay attention. You say, "Hey, you, this stuff is great. It's relevant. And you will benefit by hearing this." A great hook has three characteristics:

- It focuses the listener immediately on the key issues of the presentation.

- It grabs the listeners' attention.
- It's fast.

## Hook 'Em with a Gee-Whiz Fact

For example:

*When companies conduct a roll-out of a new type of computer hardware for their businesses, in over 70 percent of the cases, the roll-out fails. That means that the company fires the consultant hired to manage the project and they go into the market to hire another consultant.*

Or how about:

*Eighty-six percent of the population would like to see the Oreo cookie continue into the next century. Only 77 percent said the same thing about the Internet.*

## Hook 'Em with a Question

*How would you like to solve the problem of linking up buyers and sellers of media advertising time and land yourself at the center of a $150 billion industry?*

## Hook 'Em with a Clean White Shirt

John Jantson and Bruce Seeber, consultants with Kurt Salmon Associates, used a story to grab the attention of their listeners during a presentation about a new type of retail merchandising software. These software programs act as crystal balls, helping large retail chains ensure that they always have the proper inventory in place when a customer comes in wanting a particular item.

John stood and started as follows:

*I wanted to buy a nice new white shirt so that I would look nice for you here today. I went into a large department store and asked for a white button-down oxford cloth shirt in my size. The clerk was very nice, but informed me that they didn't have my size. Indeed, he told me that the shirt was in another of the company's stores across town and that they could get it for me in a few days. I told him, "No thanks" and went across the street to that store's competitor and bought the shirt. Now, I know that this has happened in your store. Well, if you have a new merchandising system, then this kind of thing shouldn't happen, because that's the kind of situation these systems are designed to prevent.*

This hook worked great for a presentation that could have begun with a dull recitation of how these computer programs work. Instead, John and Bruce worked hard to come up with a story that brought the program to life for the listeners. They scored big. After their presentation, many members of the audience stayed afterward, giving them several leads on big pieces of new business.

### What a Hook Is Not: "Hey, It's Really Great to Be Here."

The best way to begin a presentation is to just begin. Start with that story or gee-whiz fact: "Let me tell you a story about a problem we were having. . . ."

Don't start with a bunch of windy introductions. "Thank you, Mark, for that lovely introduction. I always like being here with you and your group. I'd especially like to thank the board of directors. . . ."

Barf. No one listens to that stuff. It's boring. And it adds little to the presentation.

### Don't Ever Apologize

Even worse is an apology: "I'm not accustomed to speaking." Or, "I'm sorry if I seem a little disorganized."

I recently heard a presenter who had been invited back as the keynote speaker for the second year in a row at a major convention in Atlanta. He started his presentation with a long-winded recap of what he said the previous year and apologized if there was some overlap in this year's presentation. It was as if he thought we had all taken notes last year and were wondering how he was going to elaborate!

The best way to begin is to just dive right in. Get on with it! "I'd like to start this afternoon with a gee-whiz fact. . . ."

### When Do I Introduce Myself?

Once you've finished the hook, then introduce yourself if you feel it is necessary. But keep it brief. "Good afternoon. I'm glad to be here with you today. My name is Joey Asher and I'm the president of Speechworks."

Or leave that stuff out altogether, especially if you've already been introduced. Most of the time, your listeners know who you are and where you work anyway. And frankly, they don't need to know that you're glad to be there with them. Presumably, that will be apparent if you give a good presentation. So why bother?

## Can I Use a Joke for a Hook?

"I'd like to break the ice with a joke."

I've heard many people say that, but I've never understood it. How does a joke break the ice?

Usually, jokes thicken the ice because they are neither funny nor relevant. Sometimes the joke is offensive, turning off substantial portions of the audience before the presentation begins.

We have a pretty strict policy against using jokes to begin a presentation. But if you must use a joke, then make sure it passes the Speechworks Acid Joke Test.

## The Speechworks Acid Joke Test

If you want to use a joke as a hook, the joke better meet three criteria. The joke better be:

1. **Funny.** This first requirement cuts out 95 percent of the proposed "icebreakers/jokes." These jokes are almost never funny. Usually, they are "groaners" or "eye-rollers."
2. **Relevant to the presentation.** We almost never hear jokes that are relevant to a presentation. The jokes usually consist of a throwaway line that has nothing to do with the presentation and merely serves to make the listeners wait an extra minute before you begin.
3. **Tasteful.** The joke must not have a chance of offending a single person in the entire room.

## Passing the Speechworks Acid Joke Test Ain't Easy

It's extremely difficult to meet all three criteria.

We worked with an engineer who opened a presentation with the following: "I'm going to start by telling you what Elizabeth Taylor tells her husbands: 'I won't keep you long.'"

Did the joke pass the test?

First, I didn't think it was that funny. At best, I'd call it "cute." It's more of a groaner. But let's give it a pass on the funny test.

Second, was the joke relevant? Absolutely not. In the presentation, the engineer wanted to persuade the management of a major office building to reengineer the building's HVAC and lighting system.

Third, could the joke possibly offend? Probably not. But don't dismiss this issue too fast. Odd things offend people. As a lawyer, I find lawyer jokes offensive. My wife thinks I am too sensitive. But for a time, it seemed that everyone began their presentations with lawyer jokes. I never laughed. Call me overly sensitive, but I think lawyers do great, valuable work and I don't like the derision. (Hey, quit snickering.)

Could anyone other than Elizabeth Taylor be offended by the engineer's joke? Yes! What if there were an Elizabeth Taylor fan in the room? Or maybe there was a person in the room who had been divorced multiple times and didn't find the subject humorous. What if someone was going through a painful divorce? My experience has been that high-level decision-makers often have had several divorces. Is it worth risking offending someone for a stupid throwaway line that is not really that funny? Of course not.

Unless the joke meets the three criteria, skip it and get on with the presentation.

### Keepers

1. A hook is a grabber that gets the presentation going quickly with a relevant anecdote, a gee-whiz fact, a quote, or a question.
2. Skip the introductions and just start. No one cares that you're "thrilled to be here."
3. Skip the jokes unless they're funny, relevant, and not even remotely offensive.

## CHAPTER 6

*"The worse the news, the more effort should go into communicating it."*

**– Andy Grove, Intel**

# Telling 'Em What You Told 'Em: The Recap and Wrap

Speechworks Code of Clear Communication, Section 3, Paragraph 8, reads as follows:

*"All conclusions of presentations shall comply with two fundamental principles of conclusions. First, a conclusion must build retention. Accordingly, presenters shall conclude by recapping the benefit statement (the MO) and the three key points. Second, a conclusion must be a final attempt at persuasion. Accordingly, the presenter shall conclude with a call to action, a request for business, or a motivational wrap-up story."*

### The Recap: Brought to You by the Department of Redundancy Department

The purpose of the recap is to make absolutely sure that the listener has gotten your key message. You want to be a little redundant – that's what builds retention. And just because it sounds repetitive to you doesn't mean that your listener doesn't appreciate getting a neat recap of the key points.

Do it like this:

**Restate the MO:** So, like I said at the beginning, if you want to serve your clients well, you are going to have to understand the three Rs of real estate appraisals.

### Recap the Key Points:

- First, you need to understand the different requirements an appraiser must meet to be certified at different levels.
- Second, you must understand how different types of appraisers are reliable in different circumstances.
- Third, you must understand the different types of reports issued by appraisers.

### The Wrap: Oh Yeah, One More Thing!

You don't ask, you don't get.

During the wrap, you need to ask for what you want. Remember, you're giving this presentation because you want something from your audience. You want them to do something in response to what you say. You may want them to buy your product. You may want them to buy your ideas. During the wrap, you need to ask for what you want.

### Sales Presentation: Ask for the Order

I know a sales executive for a major stock brokerage firm who advises all of his brokers to end every presentation with the following words: "I want your business." They are powerful words that have a surprisingly strong effect on a listener. If you think about it, it is a flattering thing to say to someone. It says, "I value you." More importantly, you have a far smaller chance of getting the business if you don't ask for it. So ask!

A major accounting firm wasn't afraid to ask for the

business of a major city hospital. The firm ended its presentation by recalling how two of their partners had been hit in a random street shooting and rushed to that hospital. They said that they appreciated how the hospital's doctors had been there to help them. Now, the accountants said, we want to show you how we can treat your account with the same level of care you gave our partners. They got the account.

### Informational Presentation: Call to Action
Even if you're not overtly selling, you should end a presentation by asking for a commitment from the listeners. Ask them to apply your ideas for the next 90 days. Ask them to keep their mind open to your ideas going forward. Ask, ask, ask.

When I was practicing law, I used to give a three-point presentation on what our clients needed to know about the state's trade secret laws. While I gave them an overview of the kind of information they needed to know, I also wanted them to feel free to call me if they were uncertain. So I ended the following way: "I've given you a lot of information today about trade secret laws and how they apply to you. But let me tell you the most important thing you need to remember: my telephone number. If there is any doubt in your mind, call."

### Or Try to Persuade with a Story
Sometimes it's nice to wrap up with a story that sums up your key points. We had a client who was a benefits director for a large company. His presentation explained why the cost of benefits would be going up in the organization. He wrote the following numbers on the board:

**1.8**

**365,000**

**1,100**

He said: "1.8 pounds is the weight of the baby my assistant delivered last year. $365,000 is what it cost the company to get that baby home healthy. But the family only paid $1,100. So you see, although the cost of benefits is going up, we're going to be there for you when you need us."

It was a nice way to soften the blow of a difficult message.

### Keepers

1. Recaps build retention. Be sure to restate your MO and your three key points at the end of your presentation.
2. If you don't ask, you don't get. Either ask for the order or end with a call to action.
3. You can end with a final persuasive story. But make sure it's tight and relevant.

## THE PRESENTATION CHECKLIST:
Don't Enter a Conference Room Without It

### Message Objective
- Presentation has a clear MO.
- MO explicitly states that the listener's goals (to get rich, happy, thin, or some combination thereof) will be achieved by doing what the presenter proposes or argues for during the presentation.

### Three Points
- The presentation has no more than three points in support of the MO.

### Evidence
- Each point is supported by evidence.
- Evidence is highly detailed.
- The presentation uses detailed stories and business examples as illustrations.
- Statistics are kept to a minimum and explained in a way that helps the listener see the numbers in a unique way.
- The presentation contains at least one personal example.

### Hook
- The presentation's hook grabs the listener with a gee-whiz fact, a relevant story, or a compelling question.

### Recap
- The presentation concludes by recapping the message objective and the three supporting points.

### Wrap
The presentation contains a final motivational wrap-up story or call to action.

*"God is in the details."*
**– Mies van der Rohe**

# Details, Details: Fine-Tuning the Content of Your Presentation

So now that you understand the basics of the Formula, you're ready to roll, right? You've figured out your MO. You've got your evidence down pat, the pieces are all laid out. What's next? Well, to truly give a memorable presentation, you will need to flesh out the blueprint of the Formula a bit and add a little finesse. There are some basic questions of style and structure that come up time and time again in our workshops. The following chapters offer insight on a few finer points to consider when putting together that killer presentation.

*"To do the common thing uncommonly well brings success."*

– John D. Rockefeller

# Transitions: The Mile Markers of Your Presentation

When you're on a long drive to a new place, if you're like me, you like those signs that tell you when it's 40 miles to New York City, then 30 miles to New York City, then 20 miles, etc.

The signs don't get you there any quicker, but they are somehow comforting. Those signs put your trip into some kind of context and give you a nice sense of orientation and order.

For the same reason, you need to have clear transitions between sections in your presentations. Those transitions are road signs to your listeners, telling them where you are in the presentation and keeping them oriented toward your overall goal.

### The Elements of a Good Transition

A good transition has three parts:

- A brief recap of the first point.
- An indication, either explicit or implicit, that the first point is finished.
- An indication that it's time to move to the next point.

### Transitions Ain't Brain Surgery

Remember that the sole goal of a transition is to give the listener a mental cue that one section is finished and another is on the way.

It can sound like this: "O.K., I'm done with my first point, what has happened in the past, so now I'm going to talk about my second point, what is happening now."

Or you could try to be a little smoother. "O.K., we've talked about what this tax law says today; now let's move on to point two: what will happen if the law isn't changed."

### Transitions at the End of the Second Section: Recap Where You've Been

When transitioning between points two and three of the Speechworks Formula, it's a nice touch to briefly recap the journey so far by reminding your listeners of points one and two.

"O.K., we've talked about what the law says today and what will happen if it isn't changed. Now in this last section we will talk about how we think that law needs to be changed."

### Transitions Are Most Critical for Long Presentations

Do you recognize the following scene?

Presenter is two hours into a three-hour presentation. You're not sure, but you think you've dozed off three times. You look up and there is that same fellow blabbing away. Where exactly is he in his presentation? Is he covering Internet marketing of software or programming issues?

Wouldn't you love for him to briefly recap and clearly indicate what he's going to talk about next?

Of course.

That's why transitions are critical in long presentations.

Even if you have the most riveting presentation on the day's agenda, some people in your audience may get lost. So help them out. Throw up a road sign now and then. They'll appreciate it.

### Keepers
1. Transitions are the road signs of your presentation.
2. Transition between points by stating that you've finished with one point and now are ready to move on to the next.
3. Transitions are critical for long presentations.

## CHAPTER 8

*"Don't kill your audience with bullets."*
– **Speechworks**

# Visuals:
# Don't Get Overpowered
# by Your PowerPoint

Want to see what's wrong with most business presentations today? Go to any convention and watch the keynoters. Many seem to think that the most important part of the presentation is the neat slide show they've put together with PowerPoint.

Most presenters who rely on visuals such as PowerPoint fail to understand that presenting is about connecting with an audience on a personal level and moving them somewhere. PowerPoint slides can help. But they cannot accomplish that goal by themselves.

With that in mind, we now postulate for the first time the **Speechworks Unified Theory of Presentation Visuals.**

*Visuals reinforce a speaker's message and help the audience remember key points. However, the presenter should always be the focus of the presentation, not the visuals.*

### PowerPoint Presentations Should Follow the Formula

A good PowerPoint presentation follows the Formula. Here is a simple example.

### First Slide: Hook.

The slide should show something that represents your hook. A client of ours began a presentation with a slide that said "1+1=3," representing the idea that together, the whole would be greater than the sum of its parts.

### Second Slide: Message Objective.

If your presentation is to persuade the board of directors to buy your new high-tech gadget, then your Message Objective should be something like, "By using our high-tech gadget, your business will grow." The slide could be as simple as "ACME Widget = Growth for Prospect Co." Or it could be a photograph of a prospect employee holding your gadget with a giant dollar sign in the background. Use your imagination. But the slide should be a simple representation of the idea that your product will make your prospect's company thrive.

### Third Slide: Preview/Agenda Slide.

Following the Formula, remember that once you've given your MO for your presentation, you need to preview your three points. Accordingly, the next slide should give a preview of your three key points. You don't need to have full sentences for all three points. It's better to have three key words. For example, if you're selling a high-tech piece of software, here's what your slide might say:

Wizbang Software:
• Reduces Your Costs
• Easy to Learn
• Cheap to Install

**THE HOOK**

**MO + 3 POINTS**

**POINT 1**

**POINT 2**

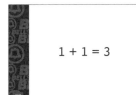

**POINT 3**

**RECAP**

**WRAP**

With these great, simple visuals, Atlanta architectural firm Jova Daniels Busby was able to reinforce its message without allowing the slides to dominate the presentation.

### Fourth Slide: Elaboration of Point 1.

This slide will be a simple representation of the key idea behind Point 1. Say you can prove that your software will save the prospect $1 million in the first two years. Then the slide should say something like "$1 million in savings over two years." Or you could show a picture of a wheelbarrow filled with money with "$1 million" written on its side. The bottom of the slide could read "Savings in First Two Years."

That's all!

Remember, the slide is to reinforce what you are going to say. You will talk in detail about how you can save them money. But you don't want to write out your entire presentation on the slide.

You deliver the message. The slide just reinforces your message.

### Fifth and Sixth Slides: Do the same for your second and third points.

### Seventh Slide: Recap. Use the same Preview/Agenda Slide.

### Eighth Slide: Wrap. This slide reinforces your close. If you're asking for the order, then maybe you have something as simple as "When Do We Start?" Or you can go for something more involved. Maybe you show a photograph of you and the client shaking hands. Maybe the next step is a site visit. In that case, show a photograph of the site.

### When Your Slides Rely on Words: Less Is More

Rely on key words rather than entire sentences.

An engineer from Nextel gave a presentation promoting the use of a new type of database software that would be a major time saver for the company. His key words for his visual aids were:

- Easier to Use
- Easier to Print Forms
- Shortens the Troubleshooting Process

That was all he needed. From there, he was able to

speak in depth about those key points. And he never had to read his slides.

If you write too much on your slides, two things happen:
- You will read your slides. Boring!
- Your listeners will read your slides. What do they need you for?

### And More Is Definitely Less
Too many words on your slides detract from your presentation.

A senior vice president from a major airline recently gave a presentation on airline maintenance procedures to approximately 300 people. His visuals were projected on two giant screens beside the podium. His slides had so much type, and the type was so small, it was literally impossible to read them. The speaker apologized several times. Ugh.

### Diatribe Against Reading Your PowerPoint
**Warning: Please skip this section if you have never read your PowerPoint slides to an audience. This will get ugly.**

Of all the presentation sins, few rank as high as reading your PowerPoint slides. You've seen this happen. The first slide goes up and the presenter turns her back on the listeners and begins reading. Uggghh!

We have a name for people who read PowerPoint presentations: Horrible, horrible, horrible presenters! If you're simply going to read your slides, then just hand them out and sit down. Your listeners can read to themselves far faster than you can read it to them.

### Slide Readers Subtract Value
You can easily calculate the exact amount of value you subtract by reading your slides. You give a half-hour presentation to twenty executives. Their time is worth approximately $250 an hour. You've just cost your company $2,500. Do the math. Unless you bring in $2,501 for that half-hour's work, your company would have been better off without you on the payroll for that time.

### Slides as Handouts

"If I don't have enough detail in the PowerPoint slides, then when my listeners keep a copy, they won't be able to remember what I said."

Don't let the visual tail wag the presentation dog. If you want the listeners to have a written record of your ideas, write a memorandum to go with the presentation. Or do a second set of slides with greater detail. Many presentation programs allow you to print a version of your slides with "speaker's notes" at the bottom. Hand out a version with speaker's notes. But don't undermine the quality of your presentation by giving your listeners something to read while you present. Hand out the detailed notes at the end of the presentation. You want your listeners watching you during your speech.

### Illustrating Statistics: Charts and Graphs

Charts and graphs present a chance for you to help your listeners see your numbers in a memorable way. Don't be afraid to be creative. Use a CD-ROM as your "pie" to illustrate percentages of CD-ROM sales. Use stacks of computer discs to indicate growth in computer sales.

**Pie Charts:** Illustrate relationships as part of a whole.

**Bar Charts:** Illustrate comparisons between numbers.

LUIGI'S: A SLICE ABOVE

### A Short Course in Visual Design

Just because you know how to operate PowerPoint doesn't mean that you know anything about design and balance when creating slides. Some tips to ensure that you don't offend anyone with your sense of style:

• No more than three font styles for a set of slides.
• No more than three colors. Dark backgrounds with bright letters are best and will hide the dust that can get on the lens.
• Put your company logo in the corner of every slide.
• For a sales presentation, include your prospect's logo on every slide.

- If you have multiple slides illustrating one of your three points, then each slide illustrating that point should reference the central point.
- Don't mix styles of clip art. Uniformity creates a nice look that doesn't offend the eye.

## Multimedia: How Fancy Should I Get?

Sure, you can make that graph slide in from the edge of the screen while you're talking. Sure, you can make your key words pop up on the screen or disappear in a flash as you talk.

But be careful. Too much animation can distract from your message. And in an age where we can recreate sheep in a test tube, the fact that you can make words pop up on a screen isn't particularly impressive.

Remember, the audience is buying you and your ideas, not your ability to create a gee-whiz slide show.

## Even the High-Tech Wizards Will Reject the Slides

We did a workshop for a high-tech cable technology company in which the participants chose to create their final presentations using PowerPoint. The PowerPoint presentation that received the most criticism from the group was the one that had all the fancy animation. "I think it distracts from your message," said one participant.

## Is There Any Evidence That This Multimedia Stuff Helps Listeners?

An entire industry has sprung up in recent years around presentation technology. *Presentations* magazine appears to exist solely as a vehicle for advertising the latest LCD projectors and multimedia software. Using this stuff, you can buy software to turn your weekly budget briefing into a fully animated multimedia extravaganza.

The question is, why?

There is absolutely no evidence that this stuff makes you connect with your listeners better than you do without it. Common sense suggests that the technology can get in the way of a good speaker.

A study conducted by *Presentations* magazine did conclude that, all things being equal, multimedia presentations aided retention better than boring old overheads. But the key phrase is "all things being equal."

Read the fine print to the study: "We tried to minimize the presenter's role . . . by coaching the presenters to deliver the information exactly the same way, whether they were using overhead slides or advanced multimedia."

In other words, their study showed only that "advanced multimedia" is, well, "advanced." But the study says nothing about whether a multimedia slide show makes a good presenter better or worse.

Actually, all those bells and whistles detract from the audience's ability to focus on the most important visual aid – you. No wonder that Scott McNealy, founder of Sun Microsystems, banned PowerPoint in his company.

### Argument with My Wife, the Fancy-Schmancy Management Consultant and Strong Advocate of Multimedia Presentations
*Location: Delta Air Lines flight to LaGuardia. Midflight.*

*Johanna:* First, I object to being characterized as a "strong advocate of multimedia presentations." Second, I hope you're not being an old curmudgeon about PowerPoint. Some people like PowerPoint.

*Joey:* (feigning ignorance) First, I'm not old. Second, I don't know what you mean.

*Johanna:* I think multimedia presentations can be helpful when you're a small person with a large audience in a big place.

*Joey:* You don't think it's better to work on a strong presentation with the presenter as the focus rather than the visuals?

*Johanna:* Of course you need a strong presentation. And you need to be good. But when you're in front of a large audience, it takes more than that to keep their attention. Plus, if you're a mediocre presenter and everyone else has nice visuals, then it's even more important to keep up with the competition.

*Joey:* I only agree with the second part of your statement. If you're a good presenter, then you don't want your visuals to step on you. I do agree, however, that if you suck as a presenter, then lay on all the visuals you can. Because if you suck, you don't want them focusing on you.

*Johanna:* That's not true. I'm not saying only use them if you stink. You can do it in a tasteful way that adds to your image of professionalism. It can make you look like a person who can use the technology well.

*Joey:* I'm not saying don't use it. I'm just saying, be careful. If you lay on all the bells and whistles, you run the danger of distracting from your core objective, which is to build a relationship with your audience. The really good presenters, by the way, rarely use all that stuff. They realize that connection happens between people. Not between people and machines.

*Johanna:* I agree with that.

*Joey:* Did I win this argument?

*Johanna:* Time to turn off your laptop. You're interfering with the landing gear.

*Joey:* How can this laptop interfere with the landing gear?

*Johanna:* The flight attendant just asked you to turn it off. Please turn it off.

## Whiteboarding: The Best Type of Visual
Along comes the ubiquitous whiteboard to save the presentation day. Whiteboards, those erasable white chalkboards, allow presenters to utilize visuals without shifting the attention away from the speaker. Indeed, if you want to reinforce a complex idea, one of the best options is the whiteboard.

## Lesson from a Whiteboarding Expert
Bob Peterson, a national sales manager at Optio Software, uses the whiteboard in many of his sales presentations to

explain how his software handles client information. "I use the whiteboard to show them a thought process that's too complicated to tell," says Peterson.

Two tips to make your whiteboarding more effective:

- Practice your whiteboarding before the presentation. Peterson practices on a yellow legal pad.
- Erase your diagram once your listeners "get it." You don't want the board to get too messy or distracting. Also, those diagrams have a tendency to remain unerased for weeks or months. You don't want people criticizing your diagram without you around to defend yourself.

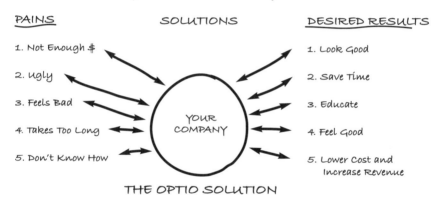

**In selling process improvement solutions, Bob Peterson starts at the left side of the whiteboard by asking for a list of the prospect's "pains" (usually he already knows the pains). Then he writes down on the right the prospect's "desired results." Then, in the middle, he points out how Optio Software delivers the correct solution.**

### Show and Tell: Demonstrations Can Be an Easy Way to Make an Audience Understand

If done right, demonstrations can make an unforgettable impression on an audience.

No one in the Washington, D.C., hearing room will ever forget Nobel Prize–winning physicist Richard Feynman immersing some rubber O-Ring material in a cup of ice water to demonstrate the cause of the explosion of the space shuttle *Challenger*.

It turned out that the insulation around the infamous shuttle O-Rings, which had properties similar to styrofoam, became dangerously inelastic at 32 degrees, the temperature on the day of the *Challenger* launch.

Feynman demonstrated the problem by immersing the material in a glass of ice water and showing how inelastic the material became at freezing point.

## The Secret to Powerful Demonstrations

To have the same high impact with your demonstrations, follow three rules:

- Rehearse the demonstration several times to make sure it works.
- Keep it simple.
- Don't demonstrate more than the listener is interested in seeing.

## The Case of the Five-Gallon Drums of Titanium Oxide

Danny Daye had a wonderfully simple demonstration to prove the value of his new Internet service, WorldWideTesting.com, when he spoke to a conference of venture capitalists. He wanted to demonstrate the value of providing on-line quality assurance for commodity products that could be purchased over the Internet.

When his turn came to make his pitch, he lumbered onstage carrying two cumbersome five-gallon drums. He stacked the identical drums on top of one another, slowly adjusting them so that the labels would face the audience.

"That is titanium oxide," he said. "This pharmaceutical-grade chemical sells for $100,000 per container. More about that later." He went on to explain how his quality assurance service was critical to giving companies confidence in the commodity products they buy over the Internet.

Finally, to close his presentation, Daye pointed to the top drum and said, "That one is pharmaceutical grade, worth $100,000. This bottom one is industrial grade, worth $320. From where you're sitting, like buyers on the Internet, how would you know the difference? With WorldWideTesting.com, you will know."

Great demonstration! It was simple, it worked – and it made a very persuasive point.

### Squint Your Eyes and See Gandhi

Or consider a simple demonstration used by Bob Jannarone, who has invented software that is able to take in streams of data and correct mistakes in the data in real time. He demonstrates the idea behind his software by handing his audience members the picture to the left and asking them what they see. Most people will say either they see just a few shades of gray or they think they see a face.

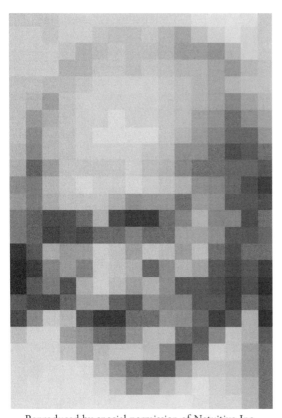

Reproduced by special permission of Netuitive Inc.

Jannarone will then take the picture and hold it ten feet away from the audience, tell them to squint a little, and then ask, "What do you see now?" In response, most will say they can see a face of a bald man.

Many will say, "It looks like Gandhi." Indeed, the image is a corrupted picture of Gandhi. Jannarone then explains, "You know it's Gandhi because your brain has the ability to fill in the missing pieces of information to create a final picture. This software does the same thing. It reads the incoming data and fills in the missing pieces to create an accurate picture in real time."

## OPPORTUNITY LOST:
## THE TRUE STORY OF HOW VISUAL OVERLOAD
## KILLED A PRESENTATION

This story is true, though the names have been changed to protect the horrible presenter and to avoid a lawsuit.

It happened at the Training 2000 conference in Atlanta in a large conference room. The speaker planned to discuss the role of the Internet in corporate training. As this was a hot topic among human resources types, the room was packed with about 300 eager conventioneers. The speaker was the president of a leading on-line training provider. Let's call him Bob.

If I were Bob, I'd think that his goal for the presentation would be to give out some valuable information, but also position himself and his company as an accessible resource for on-line training. Otherwise, why bother? He wasn't getting paid.

But Bob had no intention of developing a relationship with the audience. Rather, he intended to do a one-hour brain dump in the dark.

Bob begins by going to the microphone and uttering what unfortunately has become the de facto hook for presentations today: "Could someone please turn out the lights so that I can begin my presentation?"

Really grabs you, doesn't it? You might just as well say, "Could someone please turn out the lights so everyone can go to sleep?"

The lights go out and the first PowerPoint slide goes up. Again Bob begins to speak. I figure, now he's going to say something to get my attention.

Instead, he says, "This entire presentation is available at our company's Web site." Hearing that, about a quarter of the room got up and left. After all, the walk-outs thought, why waste time now when I can download the presentation and read it on the plane home? I'm missing another presentation across the hall.

Those who left were the smart ones. Bob spent the next hour narrating his slides. There was some interesting information, but he completely failed to accomplish the most important goal of any presentation: build a relationship with the audience and motivate them to buy his ideas.

Did anyone go up afterwards and ask him about how their company could get in touch with him? Maybe a few. But not many. I certainly didn't see any. Why? Because after an hour, Bob was still a stranger to the audience.

## Show and Tell Can Get Boring:
## Tell Them Only What They Need to Know

Remember that kid in third grade who always brought something to show and tell? Maybe it was a turtle, maybe it was an old soda can his dad found in the backyard.

And remember how this kid used to prattle on forever about the darned thing? Three rows back, you're thinking, "O.K., yeah, it's a turtle. Great. I see it. I get it. Now I'm bored. Next!"

That's the way your audience feels if you go on too long with your demonstration. Just because it's show-and-tell time doesn't mean you abandon the concepts of considering the audience's level of interest.

### Ignore the Audience's Level of Interest at Your Own Risk

Failure to consider your audience's level of interest can cost you the sale. Consider what happened to an entrepreneur who was pitching an idea for a software gadget that could diagnose illnesses. Alan Taetle, a partner in the venture capital firm Noro-Mosely, said that the entrepreneur insisted on demonstrating every little bell and whistle. "The level of detail kind of turned us off," said Taetle. "We wanted to see the overall product."

Remember to consider the WII-FM of your listener even during show and tell.

### Keepers
1. Remember that you and your presence are more important than your visuals.
2. Less is more. Fewer slides and words imprint your points in the listeners' minds.
3. A whiteboard beats PowerPoint any day.

## CHAPTER 9

*"A sudden, bold and unexpected question doth many times surprise a man and lay him open."*

**– Francis Bacon**

# Handle Questions Like a Pro

The best lesson in how to handle questions during a presentation came from that international relations geek, Henry Kissinger. Once while he was secretary of state, Kissinger had given a brief policy statement and could tell that the reporters were poised with a lot on their minds. After a pause, Kissinger said, "Does anyone have questions for the answers I've prepared?"

*The key to handling questions, be it from an audience, a*
*prospect, your boss, or in meetings:*
*Step One: Determine the Possible Questions*
*Step Two: Prepare the Answers*
*Step Three: Practice the Answers*
    *That's it, friends. It ain't brain surgery.*

## Step One: Determine the Questions

You can determine 90 percent of the questions you will get.
Here's what you do. Take out a sheet of paper and write
down questions until you think to yourself, "I won't get any
other questions than that." Then force yourself to come up
with five more questions. Rarely will you need to come up
with more than fifteen questions.

## You Really Can Guess Them All.

Political candidates always look so well prepared for a press
conference because their staffs guess 90 percent of the questions they will receive. You can do the same.

Recently, we worked with a very large computer firm as
they prepared for a big convention. This firm was introducing
a new product and wanted to make sure that the product
managers staffing the booth were well prepared for any possible questions. We had them break into two teams of five
and spend six minutes brainstorming the questions.

Interestingly, the two teams each came up with about
eight questions. But there was a lot of overlap. There were
only 12 different questions. Among those questions was
every single question the product managers received at the
booth during the two-day convention. And most people stop-
ping at the booth asked one of only two questions: "So what
is this new product?" or "What's unique about the product?"

## Don't Underestimate Q & A

In a presentation about a complex idea or product, the audience may be more interested in asking you questions than in
listening to you talk. If that's the case, leave extra time for
questions and give a shorter presentation.

We worked once with an entrepreneur who prepared a
30-minute pitch for a venture capitalist. No sooner had our

client started giving his pitch than the venture capitalist started interrupting and asking questions. My client never got a chance to give his presentation.

But that was great! The venture capitalist wouldn't have asked so many questions if he weren't truly interested in the entrepreneur's ideas.

## What About That Stick-in-Your-Eye Question You Wish They Wouldn't Ask?

You know those horrible questions that you wish they wouldn't ask? Don't include those on your list. Instead, put the answer in your presentation. When I was practicing law, we called that "getting the stink out."

One of the highlights from my brief stint as a lawyer (I only have about three legal career highlights) came when I was cross-examining a star witness for the opposing utility. The opposing counsel had failed to rehearse the witness to "get the stink out."

Briefly, the dispute in the case was over whether Georgia Power (which I represented) or a rural electric cooperative had the right to sell power to a new cotton gin in South Georgia. The gin had selected the local electric cooperative, which extended service, claiming that it had the exclusive right. The cooperative's general manager testified that the cooperative had been selected fair and square.

When he was done testifying, I was stunned. He had failed to mention what I felt was a hugely important fact. I stood up slowly and gathered my papers on the lectern. When I knew that the judge was paying close attention, I fired off my first question.

"Mr. Jones (not his real name), in addition to being general manager of the cooperative, you're also an owner of the cotton gin, aren't you?"

"Yes."

The judge visibly sat up and leaned forward. "You're an owner?" he said. Suddenly, the selection process seemed rigged against Georgia Power.

On redirect examination, the witness's attorney pointed out that the witness only owned a small portion of the cotton gin. But the damage had already been done. In my judgment, the witness never recovered his credibility. We won the case.

The lesson from that hearing room applies to taking questions after a presentation as well. If there is something you find uncomfortable that the audience may be interested in, you should take control and air the issue before someone else airs it for you. That way you can put your own spin on the issue and you retain your credibility with the audience.

## Step Two: Prepare the Answers

Once you guess the questions, take a few minutes and prepare answers for the questions. The answers should follow a basic format:

- Simple, direct answer
- Evidence

If the question calls for a simple response, start your answer with a simple response. Many questions call for a simple "yes" or "no." If that is the case, the first word out of your mouth in response should be either the word "Yes" or the word "No." Then, you should give a concrete piece of evidence backing up your answer. Tell a story, give a personal example, cite expert testimony, give an analogy, use a quote, or cite a statistic (Remember our acronym S.P.E.A.K.S. from earlier in the book?). Too often, the evidence comes first, leaving the answers unclear for a substantial period of time.

**Here's the wrong way to answer a question.**

Q. So tell us, how much does this piece of software cost?

A. Well, if you wanted to buy this piece of software last year, it would have cost only $75 a copy. The reason the cost was so low then is that it was brand new, still experimental and still gaining acceptance. So we cut the price for the early buyers. Since then, we've found that the value for the software has risen, and therefore, we have increased the price to $100 a copy.

Ending with the answer can make you sound evasive. In this case, the speaker sounds uncomfortable talking about the price of the product.

**Here's the right way to answer such a question.**
Q. So tell us, how much does this piece of software cost?
A. The cost is $100. For that price, you get all the features we've discussed. These features will save your company $1,000 in the first year or we'll refund the entire price.

Answering directly does two things. First, it satisfies the listener quickly. Second, it makes you look confident and credible.

### Step Three: Practice the Answers
Once you have the answers, *practice delivering them*. Practice each answer at least three times, enough so that it flows smoothly.
Perhaps the most neglected aspect of presenting is rehearsal. Many people will take the time to write a presentation, even brainstorming possible questions. But very few people will rehearse.
People seem to think that just thinking about the answers is enough. Well, it's not. You have to feel the words coming out of your mouth to know whether you can deliver them with authority.

### What If You Don't Know the Answer?
If you don't know the answer, don't try to fake it. Your credibility with the audience can be lost in an instant if you are caught bluffing. Instead, you can do one of two things.

**1. Palm the question off on the audience.**
Say "You know, I've never thought about that before. Does anyone here have an opinion about that?" Then open up the floor for audience participation. Instead of admitting that you don't know the answer, open the question up for the rest of the group and ask for input. But if you do this, don't turn around and restate one of the audience member's answers as your own. Again, your credibility is at stake.

**2. Admit you don't know (gasp!) and commit to finding an answer.**
During a workshop, someone once asked me whether it was

O.K. to make eye contact when speaking to people from Asian cultures. The questioner had heard that some cultures, Asians in particular, were offended by eye contact. I guessed that it could be true, but I wasn't certain.

I responded that I wasn't certain, but that I knew Nancy Newton Thomas, the former director of protocol at the Atlanta Olympic Games and a colleague at Speechworks. Nancy is an expert in international business protocol.

During a break, I called Nancy and found out that indeed some Asian cultures place far less emphasis on eye contact during conversation. But that didn't mean that you shouldn't look Asian listeners in the eye. Rather, if you're speaking to someone from an Asian country, you should realize the cultural difference and not be offended if the eye contact isn't reciprocated.

As soon as I found out the information, I reported back to my listeners.

### Getting the Questions Going

Lots of questions indicate lots of interest. When Thurgood Marshall argued the famous *Brown v. Board of Education* decision before the U.S. Supreme Court, he knew that the justices liked his arguments when they began peppering him with questions. Indeed, he fielded questions from the moment he stood up to the moment he sat down.

On the other hand, one of the sure signs that your arguments are losing is if the judges just stare at you with no questions.

The same is true of audiences. Lots of questions is good. If you don't get any questions at all, then you've probably done one of four things:
- Bored them to tears.
- Made it all sound so complicated that no one would dare ask a question for fear of sounding stupid.
- Offended someone and the audience is either afraid of you, is punishing you, or both.
- Spoken too long and it's time for lunch.

### Bore Them and They Will Ignore You During Q & A

I once heard an environmental expert speak to a utility commission on the impact of electric utility practices on the environment. He literally read a 45-minute highly technical speech to five commissioners who had little expertise in his area. Sitting through his presentation was physically painful.

When he was done, he looked at the commissioners and asked if there were any questions. Not a single commissioner moved. The expert laughed uncomfortably and returned to his seat. In this case, the commissioners were bored, afraid, and offended, all in one.

### Jump-Start the Questions

If you have carefully considered the audience's WII-FM and kept your presentation tight, you won't offend, bore, or scare them. However, it may take a minute to warm up your audience to asking questions. You can jump-start the question-and-answer session by asking the first question yourself. Try something like "The most common question I get is. . . ."

### Repeat the Question

Always repeat the question. In addition to letting the entire audience in on the question, repeating gives you a chance to formulate an answer.

### Practice Verbal Judo to Deflect Hostile Questions

Don't let a hostile questioner take control. If you get a hostile question, restate the question in a more positive way. If the question is, "Why does this product cost so much?" restate the question in a more neutral way: "The question is about how we calculate our fees."

### Or Set a Trap by Preparing a Great Response

If you know that you're going to get a nasty question, set a trap ahead of time by preparing a great response.

A famous example of this took place during the second debate between Ronald Reagan and Walter Mondale. Reagan had performed poorly in the first debate and the pundits were calling Reagan too old to be reelected.

During the second debate, Reagan was ready when a reporter asked about the age issue. "I realize that some people think that age is an issue in this race. But I'm not going to make an issue of my opponent's youth and inexperience." That line drew a huge laugh, even from Mondale, and arguably turned the tide in the election, leading to a big win for Reagan.

### Multifaceted Questions: Take One Part at a Time

"I have a question about how the software works, and how much project involvement my team will have during implementation." Don't try to answer it all at once. Preface your response by saying, "You've asked me two questions. I'll take the first question first and then I'll speak to the second."

### Cutting Off Showboaters

Sometimes you'll get a questioner who wants to take over the presentation with a lot of questions and grandstanding statements. There's a trick to handling these folks, and it takes a little psychology.

When they're going on and on, make good strong eye contact with them until they're done. Then give a good strong answer to others in the crowd, moving away from the questioner. Then as soon as you're done say, "Does anyone else have a question?"

By cutting out the eye contact and asking the audience for another question, you have cut off the showboater without humiliating him.

### End with a Recap of Your Presentation's Points

Once you're done answering questions, don't just say "Thank you" and sit down. Take control of the ending by recapping your Message Objective and your three points. It should sound like this: "So let me recap the key messages today. If you buy this product, your company is going to make more money. This product will lower your operating costs, it's easy to operate, and it is easy to install."

### Keepers

1. To be good at handling questions, guess the questions and prepare for them.
2. Never attempt to fake an answer. If you don't know, admit it and let the audience come up with an answer, or prom-

ise to get the answer as soon as possible.

3. Don't underestimate the importance of letting the audi-ence ask questions. If they have something to say, let them talk. It will make your presentation more effective.

## CHAPTER 10

*"Nothing you can't spell will work."*
**– Will Rogers**

# Dem's Some Fancy Words You're Using There, Son: Getting Rid of Jargon

Speechworks Code of Clear Communication, Section 15, Paragraph 8, contains the following provision:

*"Presenters shall carefully comb through their language to ensure that they don't use too many fancy words. Fancy words are not impressive. They are just . . . well . . . fancy. We don't understand a lot of fancy words. Where a simple word will do, use the simple word. Thank you."*

### The Speechworks Jargon Rule

*Use jargon only if you're certain that everyone in the room will understand it. Remember that the key decision-maker may simply not have heard a piece of jargon. But will she raise her hand to ask you the meaning of the word? Probably not.*

### The Problem with Jargon? It Can Make People Distrust You

A study out of England produced a startling statistic about the effect of jargon on listeners' perception. A consulting firm called Office Angels found that as many as 10 percent of those surveyed believe that people who use jargon and buzzwords are pretentious and untrustworthy. That means that out of an audience of 100 people, you lose 10 people solely because you're using a lot of jargon. You had better hope that those 10 people don't include a key decision-maker.

### Jargon Can Make You Look Stupid

The same study found that 20 percent of people who use jargon or buzzwords don't actually use them correctly. Think about how badly your credibility could be undercut if your understanding of the meaning of a buzzword differs from that of members of your audience. Even if you have the right definition and your listeners misunderstand the word, you're not helping yourself as a speaker by using words that confuse people.

Why not avoid all those problems by using simple, commonly understood terms where possible?

### Saying It without Jargon May Enable You to Make Your Point Better

Even if you are using the jargon correctly, you will probably find that eliminating it will enable you to make your point more forcefully. Consider the example of Scott Strobel, vice president of alliance partnerships at INVESCO. He wanted to convince a business partner to include the INVESCO portfolio of funds in their investment lineup. He originally had planned to include as part of his pitch the following phrase: "We try to maintain style integrity within our group of funds." By that, he meant that the INVESCO funds were all managed in a certain style.

He changed the phrase to focus on showing how the INVESCO funds had management styles that matched the needs of the listener's clients. When he was finished, the phrase was as follows: "We manage our funds in a way that offers something for everyone." He went on to explain that INVESCO offers various funds with management styles that address the needs of all types of investors, be they conservative or more aggressive.

By taking out the jargon, Strobel turned a confusing phrase into one that showed how his company's products benefited the listener.

### Or Consider the Lawyer Who Delegalized Her Speech

A lawyer for Federated Investors had to give a presentation on legal developments to the investment advisors who sold her company's products. Rather than talking about an SEC ruling prohibiting the use of "soft dollar arrangements," she connected with her audience's interests by explaining that the new ruling prohibited "waiving commissions in exchange for new business referrals." Her presentation was a huge hit because she took the legal jargon out of her presentation and spoke in terms her listeners understood.

### The "Liquidity Event" Event

Before our involvement in training of dot-coms for venture capital presentations, I was on the telephone with a friend who had a dot-com business. He kept using the words "liquidity event," as in "We are looking forward to our next liquidity event." I had no idea what he was talking about. To me, a "liquidity event" sounded like something that happens after you've had several beers. This conversation went on for about a half-hour. Finally, I couldn't stand it any longer. "What is a liquidity event?"

He explained to me that a liquidity event is any influx of cash, such as an initial public offering, a sale of the corporation, or an award of venture capital.

What was wrong with "influx of cash"?

## INTERVIEW WITH A REFORMED PROPELLER HEAD: A GEEK WHO BEAT THE URGE TO SPEAK GEEK SPEAK

Meet Steve Monsone.

He's a Macintosh service technician with his own company, Spin Multimedia. He has a ponytail, is partial to velvet pimp hats, and carries his wallet in a nifty leather pouch around his waist.

In a word, the man's a geek! But he's our geek, and that makes him special.

Indeed, Speechworks uses Steve's company to work on its computers because he's talented and because he speaks to us in our language. None of that geek jargon for Steve. We also take comfort in that ponytail. Heaven knows, you certainly don't want an old guy with a crew cut working on your computers.

"My business is communication," he says. "I understand that the client only really wants to have his machine running. Why should I throw a bunch of technology at you? You're going to be impressed when I get your machine running."

Steve also understands that communication comes hard for many geeks. "Tekkies are people who really want to be appreciated for what they do," he says. That means that they will often dump lots of nonsensical verbiage on non-tekkies. "It's narcissism," he says.

He admits that he once fell prey to that narcissistic urge. He has come a long way with his communication skills from his days when he worked as a tekkie for Apple, taking service calls from customers who needed their computers fixed.

Say a client wanted to upgrade his computer's memory. What would Steve say in those days? He admits that he would sometimes do a techno-dump on his client by saying something like, "What we need to do is put 32 megabytes of EDO RAM at a speed no less than 10 nanoseconds. And we must utilize it in pairs so it works properly with the BIOS of the CPU." In reality, he admits, all the client really wanted to know was "That's going to cost 60 bucks."

To make matters even worse, he said, many tekkies (not him) would then return to the back room with the other propeller-heads and insult the befuddled customer. "What a dumb ass!" they would say.

Steve shakes his head at the memory. "Pure narcissism," he says.

And it's great to be a geek who can speak. "A geek is someone who is intelligent, but cool," says Monsone. That's in contrast to a nerd, who is intelligent but not cool.

"I don't see any nerds getting women," he says. "Geeks nowadays get women."

Moral: Lose the jargon. Get girls.

## Language That Tries to Impress Fails to Connect
Don't throw around a bunch of jargon just to sound important. You may make yourself look silly. I recently attended a
meeting with someone who kept talking about the need to
get me an "NDA." He used the term repeatedly and I had no
idea what he was talking about. After the third time, I said
"What is an NDA?"

"A nondisclosure agreement."

Now, what this person did not know was that I was an
attorney who had spent five years drafting the documents
that he so cavalierly called "NDAs." But in all my time as an
attorney, I had never heard them called "NDAs"; we just used
the boring old "confidentiality agreement." His use of jargon
did not impress me. Rather, it made me suspect he didn't
really know what he was talking about.

## They Don't Get You There Any Quicker
Simple language connects. Everything else labels you as a
geek. (Not that there's anything wrong with that.)

## True Story from My Fraternity
A fraternity brother of mine, let's call him Curtis, planned to
call the admissions office of a medical school to inform them
how badly he wanted to be admitted off the waiting list.
"What do you plan to say?" I asked. Curtis had written out a
script and I remember it to this day. He planned to tell them,
"It is my sincere hope that a union between myself and your
institution will soon be forthcoming."

I laughed and said it sounded like a bizarre proposition
for a kinky sexual liaison. I suggested that Curtis use a more
straightforward approach: "I want to go to your school. If you
admit me, I'm coming."

## Keepers
1. Jargon can make you look insincere, untrustworthy, and
   incompetent.
2. Plain language can help you connect better with listeners.
3. The person you want to impress the most probably won't
   admit that he doesn't understand your jargon.

*"Funny is an attitude."*
**– Flip Wilson**

# Lessons from a Professional Humor Geek

So you want to be funny. The good news is that anyone can be funny.

If you don't believe it, ask Jeff Justice, a professional humor coach who has made even the geekiest, dullest people funny.

"Anyone can be funny," says Justice, who has coached over 1,000 students to do stand-up comedy through Jeff Justice's Comedy Workshoppe. "You just have to be willing to poke fun at yourself."

Poking fun at yourself is only the first of Justice's Low-Risk Guidelines for Humor During a Presentation.

### The Best Humor Is Self-Directed

"When I tell people this they often respond, 'But if I make fun of myself, people might not take me seriously,'" says Justice, who also coaches executives on how to inject humor into their presentations. "Actually the opposite is true. Study after study concludes that if you're able to take yourself lightly and poke fun at what you do, it makes people think you are extremely confident."

One of Justice's students is Charles Brewer, founder of Mindspring, which recently merged with Earthlink. In Brewer's presentation about his business, he tells hilarious stories about his adventures trying to start his Internet service provider. The stories almost always poke fun at his early stumbling as an entrepreneur. For example, Brewer claims that his original desire to get on the Internet was fueled by a desire to get weather maps on his computer.

Well . . . you had to be there.

But, trust me, to hear this computer executive claiming that his huge organization started with an insatiable desire to know the weather . . . it was funny.

### Humor Should Be Relevant to Your Presentation

Good presentation humor is always relevant. When your attempts at humor are relevant, it matters less that the joke is funny. "Even if they don't laugh at the joke," says Justice, "they're still getting the point. Indeed, they may even get the point better."

### Use Funny, Relevant Quotes

When Justice speaks about stress in the workplace, he tells the story about astronaut John Glenn, who was asked what he was thinking about as his rocket was ready to blast off. Glenn reportedly said, "I was thinking about how everything I was sitting on top of was built by the lowest bidder."

### Use a Joke from a Relevant Cartoon

When making the point that he is terrible at grammar, Justice describes his favorite Far Side cartoon, where all the Founding Fathers are sitting around writing the Declaration of Independence and Thomas Jefferson looks up and says,

"Now is it 'We the People' or 'Us the People'?" This joke is on the mark in terms of its topic (Jefferson in this cartoon also has a problem with grammar), plus it's very funny. A perfect example!

Also, by setting a cartoon up and telling it as a joke, you don't have to pay the copyright fees that you'd owe if you handed it out as part of your presentation.

### Humorous Analogies
If you have a humorous analogy, use it.

*Trying to finalize this project is impossible: it's like trying to nail Jell-O to a tree.*

### Wait for the Laugh
"Give people a chance to laugh," says Justice.

Once you deliver the funny line, you need to pause. It takes time for people to get it.

One of Justice's clients had a natural talent for humor one-on-one, but never got laughs in her business presentations. When he heard her demonstrate one of her presentations, he noticed that when she said something funny, she would just keep talking. When she started pausing for the laughter, she had to cut back her material by 25 percent because people were laughing so much.

### Pace Your Humor
Justice recommends a joke or humorous visual about every seven minutes. Anything more and you raise people's expectations too much. Your audience can start to expect too much humor and you can disappoint.

### Never Make Fun of Other People
You'll make some people laugh, but you'll also make some enemies. And even the people who laugh may start to think that you're a jerk.

### Keep Your Humor Quick
George Burns said, "Make the beginning quick, the end quick, and put the two of them as close together as possible." If you draw out a joke, Justice explains, the audience begins

to expect something truly hilarious. If you come up short, then they're disappointed.

### Don't Announce Jokes
Never begin by saying, "Here's a funny story," Justice advises. This will raise expectations that you probably can't meet.

### Keepers
1. The best humor is self-directed.
2. Make sure the joke is relevant.
3. Don't announce the joke. Just tell it.

## PART II

*"This little light of mine,*
*I'm gonna let it shine."*
**– Great American Spiritual**

# How to Deliver a Presentation with Style

It's time to talk about style. And I know what some of you are thinking. Indeed, anyone out there who deals in weighty, complex matters may be thinking it right now.

*"I am a person of substance. What matters is the actual stuff I say. The manner in which I say it doesn't matter. My stance is irrelevant. The energy in my voice doesn't matter. All that really matters is that I speak loud enough to let people hear my content. My gestures don't matter either. My eye contact doesn't matter. I don't care about style. I am SUBSTANCE MAN!"*

However, the reality, my substantial brothers and sisters, is that how we look and sound does matter. You can deliver the most important piece of information in the world, but if you don't look and sound confident when you deliver it, no one will believe you. For proof, we need look no further than a study conducted by Dr. Albert Mehrabian, a UCLA researcher. Dr. Mehrabian studied how we communicate and came up with the following statistics:

- 55 percent of the impression we make when we communicate is based on how we look.
- 38 percent of the impression we make is based on the confidence in our voice.
- 7 percent of the impression we make when we communicate is based on that glorious, geeky content.

Those numbers add up to the fact that if you want your great substance to register with your listener, then you had better pay attention to the physical style in which you present it.

A programmer friend told me that he looked down on salespeople because of their flashy style. He said he and his fellow geeks would regularly trash the sales staff at their Internet company for their allegedly phony ways. "But I also know that we did that because we felt that we couldn't do what they did." Well, you absolutely can develop your own effective presenting style without selling out and taking on the slick mannerisms of a used car salesman. Read on, brothers and sisters, and you'll see how.

## CHAPTER 12

*"Aim low – boring.*
*Aim high – soaring."*
**– Unknown**

# Finding Maximum Gary: Revealing Your Engaging Personal Style

Great news! You don't have to *develop* an engaging speaking style – you already have one. By engaging, I mean a style that can grab listeners, connect with them, and make them like you.

We call that style "Maximum Jack," or "Maximum Sara," or "Maximum [insert your first name]." Maximum You is you when you're at your most engaging. Maximum You is:

- That smile that made your wife fall in love with you.
- That eye contact you give your best girlfriend when she is opening her heart to you.
- That confident, relaxed body posture you have when you're toasting your favorite football team at the local bar.
- That energetic voice you have when you are excitedly telling your husband about that crazy thing your boss did at work today.

Everything that we discuss in the chapters in this section is designed to bring out those aspects of you the reader that constitute "Maximum You."

### Remember How Michelangelo Found the David?

Someone once asked Michelangelo how he sculpted from a single block of marble something as beautiful as his famous David. He responded that it was simple: he merely looked at the marble, saw the David, and carved away everything that wasn't the figure.

To develop your personal style, you need to see the Maximum You – and tear away everything that is not that person. You figure out how to find Maximum You and bring him or her to the presentation. You need to find that person who gets excited about sports with his friends. You need to find that person who is relaxed when chatting with a sister at the pool. You need to find that person who makes great eye contact. When you find that person and bring him or her to your presentations, you'll be a great presenter.

### Four Steps to Finding Maximum You

If you don't know how to find Maximum You, here are four steps that will help.

**Step One:** Imagine anything you're passionate about. Cooking? Fishing? Gardening? Your child's basketball games?

**Step Two:** Replay in your mind a scene in which you are discussing that passion at your highest natural level of animation.

**Step Three:** Fix that scene in your mind as a videotape that you can replay at will.

**Step Four:** Take that videotape and place an imaginary label on it. The label should read "Maximum [insert your name]."

### How We Found Maximum Gary

We had in our workshop a young executive at an Internet company named Gary. Gary had a wonderful, gregarious personality. He was the classic example of a person who could get along with everyone: big smile, twinkle in his eye, always glad to see you.

But when he stood to speak, he became "Moderate Gary." It was like he had suddenly placed a heavy weight belt on his personality. His voice became monotone. His smile was gone. It was like he was trying to fit the image of a typical corporate presenter. His presentation style was boring.

In private, Gary and I had the following conversation:

"Tell me something that you're passionate about," I said.

"Fly-fishing," he said, without batting an eye.

"And tell me about the best day you ever had fly-fishing."

He instantly drew a very detailed picture of himself in hip-waders, standing out in the middle of a Montana stream, fly-casting for trout as the sun was coming up over the horizon. Suddenly, the twinkle had returned to his eye. His voice carried a level of drama and excitement that I could feel and that made me want to go fishing.

"That's it, Gary," I said, interrupting him.

"That's what?"

"That's how you need to be when you present. Fix in your brain right now a picture of how you are right now when you're talking about fly-fishing. Make sure you remember how you feel and how it feels to talk the way you're talking right now. And talk about your work the same way."

He smiled because he instantly got it.

Maximum Gary was Gary when he was talking about fly-fishing – that was Gary at his most engaging.

### What If Maximum Gary Isn't a Slick Speaker Type?

The goal of presenting is not to be slick or perfect. The goal of presenting is to connect with the audience. The best way for you to connect is to bring out that part of your personality that has always been successful connecting with people. We're looking to find that guy who connects with his buddies.

Consider John Madden, the slightly goofy football announcer. Here is a person who is not particularly handsome. No one would ever call him slick. In fact, he's a little goofy. But he's engaging, because you get the sense that he is a real person and that he is enthusiastic. He seems a little like your wacky Uncle Buck, who loves football more than life. Just as you like Uncle Buck, you like John Madden, even though Madden isn't slick at all.

Well, that's exactly what you want when you present – you want to be that energized person who connects easily with your friends, because that person is going to engage an audience. That person is Maximum You.

### No One Said It Was Easy
Learning to be Maximum You when you give a presentation is not easy. There are two barriers to being Maximum You in front of a group.

- Nerves. How can you be Maximum You when you're shaking like a leaf? You need some techniques to deal with that problem.
- Peer Pressure. The corporate world has a collective expectation as to what constitutes a "good presenter." And that "good presenter" doesn't have the same characteristics as Maximum You. Well, ignore what they think. The best way for you to be able to connect with your audience is by figuring out what allows you to connect with audiences. That best way is to find Maximum You.

### Keepers
1. To find your best presenting style, find Maximum You.
2. Maximum You is you when you're at your best, when you're animatedly conversing with friends.
3. The best presenters are those who are able to push through the barriers to be Maximum You when in front of a group.

## CHAPTER 13

*"Failure is not an option."*
– *Apollo 13,* the movie

# How to Put the "Dot Calm" in Your Presentations: Overcoming Stage Fright

Being nervous is normal. Nerves don't hit everyone the same way, however. Here is what some of our clients have said about how they feel when they give a presentation.

- "My throat feels like I've swallowed a bag of cotton balls."
- "My heart feels like it's beating so loud, I'm sure that everyone in the audience can hear it." (That's me when I'm nervous.)

- "My hands feel clammy."
- "I feel like I have to go to the bathroom."
- "My knees literally knock."
- "I'm having trouble breathing."

Nerves affect people differently, but they always hit. Everyone gets nervous. No matter how experienced you are, you're always going to feel somewhat apprehensive. I still get nervous before every presentation. The best presenters, however, learn to control the nerves and do well in spite of their anxiety.

### First, a Few Words about Whining: Don't Do It

You've seen this scene before. Or maybe you've experienced it firsthand.

A man is introduced to an audience. He makes his way to the lectern, notes in hand. After adjusting the microphone, he says, "Uh, hi. I'm Bob Smith. I'm not used to speaking. So I'm really nervous. O.K.? But here goes. . . ."

Ouch!

How's that for a lousy way to begin a presentation? You can almost feel the audience shifting uneasily, worried that the next thirty minutes will be painful. Yet people start that way all the time.

*Don't you do it!*

If you're nervous, keep it to yourself. Three reasons:

- Unless your mom is in the audience, no one cares that you're nervous. Sorry. Deal with it.
- Telling people that you're nervous makes the audience uncomfortable. "A speaker's nerves are the most communicable disease in the world," said Louis Nizer, the late author and attorney.
- If you say nothing, chances are that no one will know you're nervous. Remember the line from *Saturday Night Live*, "It is better to look good than to feel good"? When we videotape our clients during our workshops, they are usually stunned to see that they don't look nervous even if they feel it.

## Dealing with Nerves:
## The Three Ps: Preparation, Physical Fitness, and Positive Mental Attitude

### Preparation
**Know your presentation cold.** The single best way to reduce anxiety is to practice that presentation until you know it cold. How many times do you practice your presentation from beginning to end? When we ask that question to our clients, they often say something like, "I go over it in my head a few times." That, as they say in these parts, don't feed the bulldog. You should rehearse your presentation from beginning to end until you can deliver it confidently. Three full rehearsals is a minimum. Remember the words of Abraham Lincoln: "If I had eight hours to cut down a tree, I'd spend six hours sharpening my ax."

**Practice the first few lines even more.** Usually, if you get off to a good start, your nerves will vanish. That's why you should practice that opening so often that it will sound poised – even if everyone at the head table stood up and mooned you simultaneously. I had to give a presentation to a Rotary Club once and for some reason I was extra nervous. My first words were going to be, "I want to start with a fun fact." I said that line over and over again in my head (I bet I said it 15 times while waiting my turn to speak), so that I knew when I got up, I'd get that line out just right. I was introduced and the line came out perfectly. I was rolling and things went great from there.

> Aristotle Onassis was pacing the deck of his yacht one morning when a steward approached him and asked if there was a problem. "No," Onassis is said to have answered. "I have an important meeting this morning and I'm practicing my presentation."

**Plan for the dreaded questions.** A lot of people get nervous because they fear the audience's questions. Well, plan for the questions (see chapter 9). When lawyers prepare for oral arguments, they expect to get lots of questions from the judges. How do they prepare? They spend hours working on responses to questions. You can do the same.

**Show up early and schmooze.** This is a great trick that the best presenters always use. Before the talk, introduce yourself to everyone in the room and make small talk. This accomplishes several things:

- It gets you comfortable with the audience, thereby reducing your anxiety.
- It gets the audience loosened up and more inclined to participate if you have interactive portions of your presentation.
- Chances are that you'll find someone who has a fairly close connection to you who will also make you feel comfortable. When I introduced myself to all the Rotarians, I happened to meet someone I had worked with several years earlier. Knowing he was there made me feel much more comfortable.

**Arrive early enough to check out the room and your equipment.** Nothing can make you more nervous than a bunch of surprises. Leave plenty of time to make sure that you have a place to plug in your projector. If someone else is providing the projector, then make sure you know how to turn it on. If you don't make sure it works, chances are that it won't.

**Talk to one person at a time.** Another trick is to look one person in the eye and have a little conversation with her to get yourself started. It's easy to have a conversation with one person – much less intimidating than trying to talk to the multiheaded monster that an audience can become. Just be sure not to focus on one person for too long. Have lots of miniconversations.

**Speak a lot. Presenting is like golf, tennis, ballet, and piano.** The more you do it, the better you get. Ralph Waldo Emerson said, "All the great speakers were bad speakers at first." The best speakers are the ones who work at it. If you want to get used to dealing with nerves, you need to speak a lot. If you don't have lots of opportunities, we recommend you consider joining Toastmasters International, a nationwide public speaking organization with branches in most major cities that provides its members with a wonderful opportunity to give presentations on a regular basis.

## Physical Fitness

To find out what technically happens when we get nervous before a presentation, I asked Dr. Juliet Asher, an Atlanta internist. She is also my sister.

"You recognize a situation, such as giving a presentation, as stressful," she says. "Then the brain sends a message to the adrenal glands to send out more adrenaline. The adrenaline makes your heart race faster. It makes you sweat. It puts you in a hyperalert state."

"And so you feel nervous?"

"That's right. You feel nervous."

It makes sense, she says, that you can reduce the nervous feeling by doing something to flush out that adrenaline.

"When your body is in this hyperalert state, if you direct the energy in a focused manner, such as through exercise, you use up the excess neurotransmitters and you feel less nervous."

So what can you do to get rid of those excess neurotransmitters?

**Push-ups.** Any sort of exercise will do. Walk around the block. Do jumping jacks. Billy Crystal does push-ups before a performance. "I like to break a sweat," he says. Isometric exercises work well. Press your palms together. Tense your legs. Atlantan Gary Pomerantz, author of *Where Peachtree Meets Sweet Auburn*, clenches his fists. It helps him relax before he gets up to speak during his book tours.

**Meditation.** For thousands of years, practitioners of Eastern religions have known about the physical and psychological benefits of meditation. But in 1975, a Harvard Medical School expert named Dr. Herbert Benson published a landmark book, *The Relaxation Response*, which scientifically proved those benefits. The Relaxation Response is a wonderful way to deal with stress of any kind, including stress associated with giving presentations.

If you're interested, you should read the book. But here's the quick and dirty how-to:

- Either sit or lie in a relaxed position. You want to be in a position where you can be comfortable for between 10 and 20 minutes.
- Mentally begin to feel relaxation spread through your body. Start with your feet or head and work your way through your whole body. Once you feel your feet totally relaxed, then move on to your ankles, and so on.
- Establish an easy, rhythmic breathing pattern. You should breath from your stomach. To make sure you're doing it right, put your hand over your chest. Your chest should be still, while your stomach moves in and out as you breathe.
- Clear your mind by focusing on a "mantra," any single word that you can focus on as you breathe. Pick a short word such as "one" or "relax" or "rest." Any word will do.
- Whenever your mind wanders, drag it back to your chosen word. It's hard to do. You'll find it amazing how quickly your mind will wander. But you get better with practice. And it does feels great when you can get your mind really calm.
- Start out by trying to follow these steps for about 10 minutes at a time. Work your way up to 20 minutes.

Advocates of meditation and the Relaxation Response say you should practice every day to get the most benefit. That's probably true. But even a short session 30 minutes before you give a big presentation is helpful.

### Have a Positive Attitude

**Act cool and you'll be cool.** Regardless of how you feel, you need to act positive about your presentation. Amazingly, this will help you feel less nervous. Psychologists have known for years that feelings follow actions and not the other way around. The famous psychology geek William James wrote:

"Action seems to follow feeling, but really action and feeling go together; and by regulating the action, which is under more direct control of the will, we can indirectly regulate the feeling. . . . So, to feel brave, act as if we were brave, use all of our will to that end, and a courage-fit will very likely replace the fit of fear."

All of which is a very geeky way of saying, "You really can fake it till you make it."

**Positive mental imagery.** Every *Caddyshack* geek has his favorite line. Mine is when Chevy Chase implores his golfing protege to "See the ball. Be the ball." Indeed, athletes have improved their performance for years with positive mental imagery. Basketball geek/great Bill Russell would play entire games in his head before ever walking out on the court.

Similarly, you can calm your nerves by visualizing yourself being a superstar when you give a presentation. Hear the audience laughing at your clever lines. See your listeners leaning forward in their seats, hands raised eagerly to ask questions. Those positive thoughts will gird you for success.

**Slap yourself in the face.** The last word on this issue comes from Cher in the movie *Moonstruck*. Nicolas Cage's character tells Cher's character that he is in love with her. Cher responds by slapping him in the face and saying, "Snap out of it!"

Ultimately, you need to snap out of any fear you have. Your audience wants you to be great; your company wants you to be great; you want to be great. Don't let your fear hold you back. You've rehearsed. You've imagined yourself doing great. Now go out there and be a superstar.

As they said in the movie *Apollo 13*, "Failure is not an option."

## Keepers
1. The best way to deal with nerves is to rehearse your presentation several times.
2. Practice physical relaxation techniques such as exercise and meditation.
3. Snap out of it. "Failure is not an option."

*"Nothing great was ever achieved without enthusiasm."*

**– Ralph Waldo Emerson**

# How to Sound Like a Winner: Energize Your Voice

Mark Twain once lost his cufflinks.

The story goes that Twain furiously tore his bedroom apart, spewing forth a disgusting river of some of the foulest language imaginable. After living with Twain for many years, his wife had finally heard enough. So she went to their bedroom and stood in the doorway, waiting and listening as her husband rifled through his drawers. After Twain finally stopped swearing, she began repeating back to him every foul word she had heard – in a monotone.

Twain listened quietly with a bemused expression. When she was finished with her little demonstration, he smiled and shook his head.

"Darlin'," he said, "you got words, but you ain't got the music."

## Do You Have the Music in Your Voice?

Many people with high levels of expertise have the words, "but they ain't got the music." Sure, you know your subject matter. And many of you may think that knowledge and information is enough. Well, that's just not the case. You need to have energy in your voice. Otherwise, you will fail as a communicator.

## Why Do You Need Enthusiasm in Your Voice?

Voice energy is the magic ingredient that can almost single-handedly turn you into an engaging speaker. If you have rotten gestures, it's O.K., as long as you have great voice energy. If you punctuate your language with distracting filler words such as "uh" and "you know," you can get away with it as long as your voice conveys excitement. You can even keep an audience entertained with a poorly organized message, so long as your voice conveys energy and passion.

## It's the Passion That Wins Audiences for Ted

Consider media tycoon Ted Turner. By many measures, he's a lousy speaker. I heard him speak once. His presentation rambled. I cannot tell you a single point he made, though I think there might have been something in there about the environment. Every other word out of his mouth was "Uh."

But he was fascinating to listen to.

Why?

Because his stream-of-consciousness rambles were so enthusiastic. His enthusiasm truly was infectious, and he received a sincere round of applause.

## So What Does an Energetic Voice Sound Like?

How about:
- Your daughter when she finds an Easter egg.
- Clint Eastwood in *Dirty Harry* saying, "Go ahead. Make my day."

- A three-second pause for emphasis right after somberly announcing how disappointed you were in last quarter's sales figures.
- Your voice when you're excitedly telling your husband about how you just discovered a new way to solve a problem at work.
- Jack Nicholson in *A Few Good Men* saying, "You can't handle the truth."
- Your voice when you're telling your friends a favorite fishing story over beers.
- Albert Finney in *Network* shouting, "I'm mad as hell and I'm not going to take it anymore!"
- Your voice when you're happily gossiping with girlfriends.
- Oprah at all times.
- Maximum You.

### How Do You Have Energy When You're Nervous? Have You Considered Doing Impressions?

Most poor presenters have difficulty conveying enthusiasm and energy because they're nervous. "My heart's pounding. My hands are sweating. My mouth is dry. And you want me to convey a sense of excitement?"

Well, yes. But there's an easy way to accomplish it. You need to trick your voice into sounding as if you are excited. Remember how to find your Maximum You? (See chapter 12.) Go through those steps again and listen to the voice you use when you're at your most engaging. Then make a concerted effort to act and talk that way.

### How to Fake It Until You Make It: How to Mechanically Inject Energy

O.K. You're having trouble finding Maximum You. And you're having trouble getting that energy into your voice. There are some mechanical ways to inject energy. The trick is to make your voice become like a roller coaster; you want it to rise and fall, speed up and then slow down. Whatever you do, don't allow your voice to sound like a long, slow freight train. The idea here is to create some drama.

## Here's an Exercise That Will Help Your Voice Project a Sense of Drama

In our workshops, we have our clients stand to read the following sentences as directed. You get more out of it the more you try to ham it up.

READ LOUDLY
VOLUME ADDS EMPHASIS TO AN IMPORTANT WORD OR PHRASE.

Read softly
A whisper acts as a magnet and pulls the listener to you.

*Read fast*
*Speaking rapidly excites and energizes an audience.*

Read Slowly
A slow rate of speech creates a mood of awe and wonder.

Tape-record yourself and play it back. Many of our students are stunned to learn that their "fast" voice sounds exactly like their "slow" voice and their "loud" voice has the same volume as the "soft" voice. If that's the case, then you need to learn to create a noticeable range in the speed and volume of your presentation voice.

## Dynamic Range: Pair Off for Extra Drama

You don't want to be just loud or just soft, though. We had a client who spoke loudly all the time; he thought that more energy meant more volume. In fact, he did sound enthusiastic when you first met him and for the first couple of sentences. But after a few minutes, it just seemed as though he thought all his listeners were deaf.

The drama in your voice comes from speaking both loudly and softly, both fast and slow, all in the same thought. Here's another exercise we do with our clients. Read the sentences as directed.

*Read the first half loud and the second half soft with a long pause in the middle:*

ARE WE GOING TO TAKE ALL THIS WORK . . . and throw it down the drain?

*Read the first half fast and the second half slow with a long pause in the middle:*

*I can't tell you how many times I've told this to my clients during depositions . . .* listen to the question carefully before starting to answer.

## Or Try Carrying around a Tape Recorder for a Couple of Days

When you have a big presentation coming up, carry a tape recorder around for a few days, practicing sections of your speech. Try saying different parts with differing levels of passion. Play the tape back to see what sounds best. Remember, the goal is not to be reserved – the goal is to show passion and sell ideas. Which voice sounds the most believable and passionate?

## Top Four Voice Energy Problems, as Described by Speechworks's clients

1. **"I can't speak with any passion because I don't feel any passion."**

We don't believe people when they tell us this. Our experience with people who show no excitement or enthusiasm is that they are actually embarrassed to "let it all hang out" and be themselves in front of an audience.

We worked recently with a woman from a big money management firm who claimed she simply was unable to express passion when she gave a presentation because she felt no passion about anything.

When we took her into a private room, we forced her to artificially hit a "15" on a passion scale, where a "10" constitutes total passion.

In other words, I said, "Blow my doors off. Just do it. I promise I'll only laugh at you a little bit."

She laughed and finally let it all hang out. She tried to hit a 15, but only reached a nine. When we videotaped her, she was stunned to see that what felt ridiculous and "over the top" to her inside actually looked fine to an audience. She didn't look ridiculous. She just looked enthusiastic.

### 2. "But my voice is loud."

Men, and to a lesser degree women, often think that being a good presenter means speaking loudly. Remember, energy is not volume. You can show excitement and passion with a whisper. Former president Bill Clinton once captivated a group of 60 women from the American Jewish Federation by speaking so softly that they had to lean in close to hear him. Sometimes a soft voice is just the right touch. But you never want to sound like you're shouting. Rather, you want to be excited, like you are during an enthusiastic dinner conversation with close friends.

### 3. "I'm just a soft-spoken person."

This is also generally just an excuse for being scared to "let it all hang out." We hear this mostly from women (many of whom were taught as girls never to be too loud), but sometimes from shy men.

Again, the solution is to engage in role-playing.

Recently we had a male attorney in our workshop who was a very soft-spoken person. To help him get out of his shell, we had him play the role of a furious football coach at half-time.

Here is what he said and did:

"Gentlemen, that first half was the sorriest display of football [now shouting] I HAVE EVER SEEN. [Long dramatic pause] Jones, [softly] how many times have we run that pass pattern with you? [Long pause] And Smith, DO YOU KNOW HOW TO TACKLE? [Long pause. Now softly] Well, do you?

Indeed, this attorney did have some passion in him, as we plainly saw. Now he just needed to bring it out once in a while in a real presentation.

### 4. "My voice becomes squeaky when I get nervous."

When people are nervous, sometimes the adrenaline can

cause their vocal cords to tighten. What you need to do is learn to relax your vocal cords. When our clients have this problem, we have them talk while holding a pencil between their teeth. When you do this, you're forced to drop your jaw, which loosens the vocal cords and lowers your voice.

Try it. It works.

Now you will know how your jaw should feel when you give a presentation. Of course, remember to put down the pencil before you're introduced.

### More Fun with the Tape Recorder

To learn to inject drama, nothing is better than a little imitation. Tape-record a favorite monologue from a movie or television program and transcribe it. Try any closing argument from *The Practice* or maybe Michael Douglas's "Greed is good" speech from the movie *Wall Street*. Anything from Shakespeare will also work. Practice reading the speech into a tape recorder with as much drama as you can muster. Listen to it and then do it again and again until you get all the dramatic ups and downs just right.

### Or, How about a Little Fun with Your Voice Mail?

How do you sound on voice mail? Practice leaving yourself a voice mail. Play it back. Is your voice energy there when you leave messages? It better be.

### A Final Word on Voice Energy: It's Only the Most Important Thing

For most people, lack of voice energy is the single most significant barrier to becoming a great presenter. Most people get up in front of a group and become reserved; they pull in and don't present the audience with a particularly energetic voice. If you can work on only one presentation skill, 90 percent of the time it should be voice energy. If you don't sound passionate, your presentation simply will not come across as exciting, regardless of its substance.

### Keepers

1. Passion in your voice is the single most important factor in getting your audience excited about your ideas.

2. To convey passion, make sure that you're always speaking as if you were speaking to friends during an animated dinner conversation.

3. You can simulate passion if you don't feel it by teaching your voice to simulate a roller coaster as you speak.

## CHAPTER 15

*"A sage thing is timely silence."*
**– Plutarch**

# When Silence Really Is Golden: The Pause

Sitting by the pond with my fishing pole, I'd often ask my grandfather (my fishing partner in those days) why I wasn't catching anything.

"You're not catching anything," Grandpa would say, "because you're holding your mouth the wrong way."

Sometimes the same is true with speaking. Sometimes the best way to hold your mouth . . . is closed. Sometimes silence – a good long pause – can go a long way toward reeling in an audience.

As Mark Twain said, "No word was ever as effective as the rightly timed pause."

## The Pause: Highlighting the Wonderful, Versatile Tool of Silence

The pause is one of the best tools in the speaker's arsenal because it can do so much for you, while making you look so confident.

The pause:

- Builds a sense of drama as the silence fills the room.
- Gives you a chance to think of your next thought.
- Replaces filler words like "um" and "you know."
- Emphasizes a key word or phrase.
- Lets the listeners absorb your idea.
- Gives you a chance to breathe.

## The Key to Great Pausing: Getting Comfortable with the Sound of Silence

If you're not used to pausing, remaining silent can be almost physically painful. And even the shortest pause can seem like an eternity.

The key to learning to pause is to practice holding the silence twice and even three times as long as feels comfortable. You'll be surprised at how long you can pause and still keep your audience rapt.

During our workshops, we ask our clients to recite the following, punctuated by good long pauses.

"A pause shows poise . . . control . . . confidence . . . use it . . . master it."

Inevitably, several of the clients will read the sentence with virtually no pauses at all.

"How did those pauses feel?" I will ask.

"They felt pretty good," the client will respond.

"Well, you didn't pause at all."

The client will usually look at me like I'm nuts, certain that their pauses were quite long. But their classmates will tell them the same thing.

To really master the pause, you need to train your ear to understand that you can pause a long time without sounding silly.

## O.K., You Want to Know Exactly How Long to Pause?

How about six seconds? Pause for six seconds. Long enough to say, "Did you get that?" and then wait a couple more seconds.

### Confessions of an F-Wad: A True Story of How to Eliminate Filler Words Like "Um" and "You Know."

I have a confession.

For years I was an F-Wad.

It's true. I was a "Filler Word Addict," also known as an F-Wad. You may be familiar with my addiction. I was hooked on words such as "like," "you know," "uh," "umm," and "well." I used them all. It was horrible. It seemed that I couldn't get through a sentence without uttering a filler word.

The words ate away at my appearance of confidence like a virus.

Like many F-Wads, the core of my problem was fear. As I thought of my next sentence, I hated the silence. I hated that silence like Sun Microsystems hates Microsoft, like Mac users hate Windows, like . . . well, you get the idea. The thought of just a few seconds passing by without my voice filling the air horrified me.

But then I grew determined to make the silence my friend. How did I do it? Three steps.

1. I resolved to be conscious of the problem for a few weeks. I didn't pick any particular number of weeks. But three should be enough for any serious F-Wad.

2. I sensitized my brain to know when I was using filler words. Most people who use filler words don't even hear them coming out of their mouths. I simply resolved to be aware that I was using the words and to hear them as I said them.

3. Once I was aware that I was using the words, I worked on closing my lips whenever I sensed I was about to utter one.

Before long, whenever I got to a point in the conversation where I couldn't think of what I was going to say next, I'd consciously keep my mouth shut and remain silent while I thought about what to say. At first it was awkward. That silence remained intimidating. But gradually I became comfortable with the silence and realized that allowing a pause in the conversation showed confidence.

Try it, my fellow F-Wads. You have nothing to lose but your "uhs."

## You Don't Talk Too Fast – You Probably Don't Pause

During our workshops, we ask people whether they think they talk too fast. Inevitably, several people raise their hands.

Well, next time someone tells you that you talk too fast, you tell them that you absolutely do not talk too fast. What you probably don't do is pause.

The fastest speakers rarely talk more than 200 words a minute. Yet we can all comprehend speech spoken at a rate of more than 300 words a minute.

But if you talk nonstop without pausing, your listener can get the sense that you're racing through your material. While they can hear all your words and can understand you, they may not have time to process all your ideas.

That's why it's always good to inject a few pauses. It gives you a more deliberative presence and gives the listener a chance to contemplate your ideas before you move on.

## Pause to Hide Nerves at the Beginning of a Presentation

You've just been introduced. Inside you're shaking like a leaf. If you're like most people, you want to start talking the moment you get to the lectern.

Instead, pause. Give the audience a confident, friendly smile. Take in the view for a moment. Then start talking.

That pause makes you look extremely confident, like you're in total control of the space and are willing to make everyone wait a few moments before you begin.

You may feel nervous inside but you'll look great. And, in the game of presenting, how you look counts a lot more than how you feel.

## Pause to Highlight a Key Point

The pause is a dramatic tool. Use it to be a little dramatic.

I worked with a large software firm that was promoting their product's ability to quickly interface with other products. Here's one way they emphasized the value of their product.

*It can take six weeks to customize most warehousing software. (pause) That can cost you thousands of dollars. But our product can be ready for you to use (pause) in only one day.*

The pause is a wonderful way to dramatize the special benefits that you or your product offer.

## Pause to Remember What You Were Going to Say

The great thing about a pause is that it is such a cool way to collect your thoughts.

You've forgotten your next point? Don't stare at the ceiling and say, "Uh, I've lost my train of thought." Instead, turn your head downward in a contemplative pose and silently gather yourself.

When you start talking again, no one will know that you were frantically trying to remember what to say next. They'll just think that you look cool and poised.

## Pause as a Closing Technique

An engineer whom we know sells lighting upgrades for large buildings. He goes into a building and tells the management that he can cut their lighting bill in half if they will hire him to replace the old lighting fixtures.

It's truly a great product. But we find his closing technique kind of interesting. He relies on the pause.

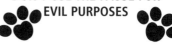

## DON'T USE THE PAUSE FOR EVIL PURPOSES

As you now know, the pause is a thing of great beauty. But in the wrong hands, it can be used for evil. Don't be one of those people who abuses the power of the pause.

Pause abusers use silence to intimidate. I was working once with a sales rep, reviewing a videotape of a pausing exercise. As we were talking, he confessed that he hated his boss.

"He constantly tries to intimidate," the sales rep said.

"What does he say?"

"It's not what he says. It's what he doesn't say. I'll say something to him and he will just stare at me, saying nothing."

That sales rep worked for a pause abuser.

When I was practicing law, the silent treatment was a well-known method for intimidating opposing counsel. During a negotiation, you'd make an offer and the opposing counsel would say nothing. That pause was a silent way of saying, "Pound sand, lawyer boy!!"

**USE THE PAUSE.
BUT DON'T BE A PAUSE ABUSER.**

He gives his presentation and then asks his prospect for the order by saying something along the lines of "If you like everything I've said, I'd like to send the contract over tomorrow."

"And then I shut up," he says. "Whoever talks next loses."

It may not be for everyone. But there's one sales engineer who has learned the power of the pause.

## Keepers

1. Use the pause to show confidence.
2. Replace filler words with the pause.
3. Use the pause to emphasize key points.

## CHAPTER 16

*"A smile is a handshake with your face."*
**– Speechworks**

# The Ol' One-Two: A Smile Coupled with Eye Contact

Call it the Ol' One-Two.

One is eye contact.

Two is a smile. A sincere smile.

That simple combination is the strongest nonverbal communication tool for connecting with any listener. When you hit someone with the Ol' One-Two, it's almost impossible for him or her not to like you.

## Sam Walton Knew About the Ol' One-Two

Perhaps the greatest retailing geek of all time was Sam Walton, creator of Wal-Mart. In his autobiography, he tells about how he came to be elected to several student government offices at the University of Missouri, even though he was from Arkansas and knew few people on campus.

His campaign strategy was as follows: When walking across campus, every time he saw someone (anyone) coming down the path towards him, he'd make eye contact with them and smile. Then he'd say something nice like "Hello."

The result? His fellow students elected him to several offices.

That's the power of the Ol' One-Two. Something about eye contact and a smile builds relationships.

**ANOTHER SEMISERIOUS SPEECHWORKS MONEY-BACK GUARANTEE**
If you use the Ol' One-Two with your listeners and they still dislike you, return this book to Speechworks for a full refund. Please include proof that your smile is sincere. Also, to get the refund, include a Polaroid of your smile.

## The Ol' One-Two Will Do More Than Make You an Engaging Presenter: It Could Change Your Life

If you learn nothing else in terms of facial expression, learn the Ol' One-Two. As much as anything else in this book, the Ol' One-Two can do more than make you a great presenter; it can change your life.

I know, because it changed mine.

As a true geek at Cornell University, I remember the first woman who gave me the Ol' One-Two. I was so taken aback, I looked around to make sure she wasn't looking at someone else. When she giggled, I asked if maybe she wanted to have lunch with me at Sa's, a popular sandwich shop in Collegetown. We split a Tuna Moon sub. A few years later, I married her. Many years later, we have three kids.

That's the power of the Ol' One-Two.

## The Ol' One-Two, Part One: Eye Contact

To find out why eye contact builds trust, I recommend that you go to the original source of this piece of wisdom, your mom. After all, wasn't she the first person who told you to look people in the eye when you talk to them? My mom said, "I guess it's just human nature. We tend to trust people when they look at us directly." There you have it. I know that eye contact builds trust because my mom told me so.

## How to Make Eye Contact during a Presentation

CBS anchor Bryant Gumbel says that when he talks to millions of people on television, he actually acts as if he's only talking to one person. And he looks right at that one person. That's what you need to do as well when you give a presentation. Focus on one person at a time and hold eye contact with that person through a thought. Your entire presentation should take the form of random miniconversations with as many individuals in the room as possible. If you're speaking to a small group (less than 25), you should try to make eye contact with everyone in the room at least once during your presentation.

## Guess Why You Should Never Read a Speech or Your PowerPoint Slides

In the Speechworks Communications Code of Crimes Against Audiences (the companion law to the Clear Communications Code), reading a speech or a PowerPoint slide is an offense punishable by a three-day wedgie. People who read their speeches or their PowerPoint slides are terrible presenters, largely because they never connect with their audience. And they never connect because they never make eye contact with anyone.

## Play the Eye Contact Game

Here's a game you can try with your friends to learn how to give sustained eye contact during a presentation.

- Seated in chairs around the room, have each of your friends put their hand in the air before you begin.
- When you begin speaking, make eye contact with one of your listeners and hold it.
- The listeners should not put their hand down until they feel that you have really connected with them.

- The game is over when you get every one of your friends to put their hands down.

You'll find that it takes quite a bit of work to get those hands down. You really need to hold that eye contact for several seconds to give the listener the sense that you've connected.

### The Eye Contact Paradox: Connecting with Huge Audiences One Person at a Time

The Eye Contact Paradox is that in order to connect in a personal way with huge audiences (say 50 people or more), you need to make eye contact and have intimate conversations with only a few of the audience members.

Let's say that you're speaking to 300 people. There's no way that you can make eye contact with each person in the room. Nor should you try.

But you do need to make sure that you make good eye contact with individuals in all sections of the room. Here's how to do it. Find the individuals to make eye contact with by using a "Z" shape:

- Start by connecting with someone in the back left of the room.
- Then move to the back right and connect with someone there.
- Moving down the Z, next connect with someone in the approximate center of the room.
- Then find someone in the front left.
- Then the front right.

By connecting with individuals in each section, listeners in all corners of the room will get the sense that you were talking to them individually. And your delivery will be very intimate.

### Avoid Grazing with your Eyes

Grazing is when you never really look at anyone for more than an instant. Instead, your eyes graze over the tops of everyone's heads. It's not surprising that grazers never feel truly connected with an audience because they really don't connect with anyone.

Worse, grazers sometimes get terribly distracted. If you're not making eye contact, you could get distracted by people getting up to leave or maybe the waiter juggling a load of dishes.

Most importantly, the audience can sense when you're not concentrating on them. If that happens, you're lost.

## What Happens When Someone Refuses to Look Back

The following situations could happen to you because they've all happened to us in our workshops:

- A woman sits in the corner of the room, looking down, refusing to look at you when you look at her.
- An old man sits in the front row, slumped down with his eyes closed.
- A younger man sits to your left, scowling and smirking at what you say.

What do you do?

It's simple: don't look at those people. Instead, look at the people who are interested. It's easy to get rattled by individuals in the audience who seem to be openly rejecting you. But you have to be there for all your listeners. You can't allow yourself to get distracted, so focus on the ones who are interested.

## Those Nasty Looks May Have Nothing to Do with You

You may find out that the unreciprocated eye contact isn't a reflection on you. More likely, it's the listener's problem.

A woman refused to make eye contact with me during a presentation workshop, but it turned out that she had had a problem with eye contact all her life. Speaking to her later, I learned that she never looked anyone in the eye, ever.

Another time an elderly man appeared to be sleeping. Speaking to him later, I learned that he loved the presentation and was listening to every word. He simply had an odd way of showing his fascination.

Another time I had a scowler, a young man who smirked repeatedly at the points I made. As the workshop continued, the Speechworks coaches worked very hard to connect with this person. We couldn't.

Oh well. You can't win 'em all.

## The Ol' One-Two, Part Two: The Power of the Smile

We had a woman in our workshop recently who was a chief financial officer for a major hospital in South Carolina. She was very soft-spoken. But as she spoke, she had this gentle but sincere smile. Not only did her lips smile, her eyes did, too. That alone made her a very engaging presenter. That's the power of a great smile.

### AN AMBASSADOR'S LESSON IN EYE CONTACT

Few presenters connect with their audiences as well as former U.N. Ambassador Andrew Young. Young, a civil rights leader who also was a U.S. Congressman and Atlanta mayor, told me a story of the first time he learned how important eye contact is for making that connection.

As a minister in his early 20s, he always preached from prepared notes. But as he was preparing to preach to a church in Beachton, Georgia, a deacon, seeing his notes, pulled Minister Young aside. "The Primitive Baptists come to worship with us," the deacon explained. "And they believe that if anything is on paper, then the devil has something to do with it. They want to know that whatever you say comes from your heart, not from a piece of paper."

So Young put away his notes and continued on to a remarkable career.

The lesson: Instead of reading your speech from notes, look your listeners in the eye to ensure that you come across as sincere.

### You May Think You're Smiling, but Are You Really?

If you can't connect with people with a genuine smile and eye contact, there may be something wrong with your smile. Check out your smile in the mirror. It's that thing where the ends of your mouth point upwards away from the ground. The eyes tend to twinkle and your teeth will show.

This sounds somewhat facetious, but many people in business truly don't know how to smile. We had a lawyer in our workshop once who, despite his best efforts, could not smile. The best he could muster was a little smirk.

### Debug Your Smile: Steal a Trick from the News Anchors

If you're having trouble with the smiling thing, here's a two-step fix.

Videotape yourself giving a speech while trying to smile. Simply seeing how little you're smiling can help a lot. When I first saw myself on camera, I was stunned to see how serious I looked.

Give the presentation again, but this time paint a phony, gigantic smile on and speak through the smile. When you watch the tape, chances are that what felt like a phony smile actually looked quite good.

This is one of the oldest tricks in television news, according to Marilyn Ringo, a Speechworks coach and former CNN *Headline News* anchor who still does frequent television appearances. TV people put on a big smile, and then force the words out between their grinning teeth. It may feel strange, but it looks genuine.

### But Isn't Smiling When You Present Kind of Phony?
No!

Remember, your goal when you communicate or give a presentation is to be Maximum You. When you're excited about something and talking about it with friends, chances are that you're smiling as you speak. It's only when you get nervous that you revert to that unsmiling, unconnected person called "Nervous Presenter You."

Smiling when you speak is a *natural* thing.

### "But I'm Not a Smiley Person. I Rarely Smile."
Now, if you truly never smile – even when you're relaxed and conversing with friends – then put down this book and return to the bookstore's self-help section, see a shrink, or maybe your priest. What you evidently need is something that this book can't help you with.

I'm serious. Put down this book now and call your rabbi. You may need some help to turn that frown upside down.

### Of Course, You Can't Smile All the Time: Other Facial Expressions
Of course, you don't want to smile all the time. You want to put some variety in your face, just like you want variety in your voice. You have over 80 muscles in your face, capable of making over 8,000 facial expressions. Use those expressions. Use your eyebrows. Purse your lips. Squint your eyes. Be expressive.

Try this exercise:

Stand in front of a mirror and read the following sentence: "I'm going to give you some information that will make you rich." Read it five times, but using facial expression alone, convey anger, fear, joy, sadness, and paranoia. You have lots of power in your face. Use it.

## Keepers

1. Eye contact coupled with a smile is an unstoppable combination to build a positive rapport with any person.
2. When giving a presentation, hold your eye contact with each person through an entire thought. Don't graze.
3. Force yourself to smile when you speak. It warms your presence.

## CHAPTER 17

*"Come before your listener wearing boots and spurs, not bedroom slippers."*
**– Speechworks**

# "You Look Maahhvelous": How to Have Great Presence

You know you've done this. The elevator closes – it's one of those mirrored elevator doors – and you take a furtive glance at how you look.

Well, how do you look?

If your stance were a handshake, would it be firm and confident? Or would it be a cold fish?

How you carry yourself says a lot about you. You want to carry yourself in a way that conveys two things to the listener: confidence and openness.

And the great thing about it is, you can fake it.

**How to Look Confident Even If You Don't Feel Confident**

"But I don't feel confident."

That's something we hear constantly in our workshops. Indeed, it's normal not to feel confident when standing in front of a group. You're nervous.

But you absolutely can look confident, and no one will ever know how you feel.

Here's what you do.

- **Stand up straight.** Just like your mother told you. Are your shoulders back? Is your chest out?
- **Place your feet shoulder-width apart with one foot slightly ahead of the other.**
- **Shift your weight slightly toward your front foot.** Weight forward looks more confident than weight back. Look in the mirror and say the following two times, once with your weight forward and once with your weight on your heels. "I want you to invest $1 million in my business." Which is more convincing?
- **Leave your arms by your sides with your hands hanging open.** Arms at your sides looks confident and open. Cross your arms, clasp your hands, or do anything that hides part of your body, and you look defensive. Be open, not closed.
- **Relax.** Don't stand like a soldier. You want to be open and confident, but not stiff and foreboding.

Here's what you want to look like when you're in the "neutral" position:

Here is a more defensive-looking pose: head tilted, hands clasped.

## The Presence Concept: Openness to the Listener

Everything about your presence should convey a sense of openness to the audience and your listeners.

- That's why you have your hands at your sides, rather than crossed over your body. Arms crossed conveys a sense of being closed to the listener.
- That's why you lean forward. Leaning forward gives the sense of being connected to the audience.

If you don't convey a sense of being open with your listeners, you will not connect as well as you could otherwise.

## "Now I'd Like to Introduce. . . .": How to Take the Stage Like a Pro

Watch the Academy Awards to see how to strut on stage when you're introduced. "And now, introducing Mel Gibson, to announce the award for best supporting cinematographer in a foreign film."

Here comes Mel. He struts out on stage in a tuxedo and cowboy boots. He's looking at the audience with a slight smile. This is a star!

You can do the same. Just be like Mel.

Stride out with purpose, like you're wearing boots and spurs. Don't shuffle out on stage like you're in bedroom slippers.

Make eye contact with someone in the audience.

Smile.

When you get to center stage, stop and pause. Don't say anything for a couple of seconds. Just pause and take in the view. Make 'em wait for a moment.

Then take a step forward and begin.

## And Before Leaving, Wait for the Standing O

When your presentation is done, don't be in a rush to sit down. Wait for the applause. Smile and accept the adulation. Be confident.

## Seated Presence: Beat the Corporate Schlub Slump – Be Like Katie and Cokie

Slouch down in your seat.

Lower.

Lower still.

I want you so slumped down that the top of the meeting table is almost at eye level.

Now you're sitting in the position that much of corporate America assumes during meetings.

We call it the Corporate Schlub Slump, and it conveys not only a lack of confidence but an aggressive sense of boredom.

How do you convey confidence and openness while seated? Watch news anchors Katie Couric and Cokie Roberts.

Here's what they do.

- They sit up, with their backs against the back of their chairs.
- They keep their backs straight.
- They lean slightly forward.
- They have their arms up on the table. (With your arms below the table, you look like a talking head. If there is no table, rest one arm on the arm of your chair and put the other in your lap. Both arms on your chair looks a little stiff.)
- They keep their arms open as opposed to crossed on their bodies.

Once again, the key is to convey a sense of openness to the listener.

## Take Control of a Meeting by Standing Up

There's a trick that will instantly put you in control of any meeting. When it's your turn to talk, stand up.

Go up to the whiteboard to discuss an issue. When you're up, you have the floor.

Stand up to give out your handouts and remain standing while you discuss your points.

Don't sit down until you feel you've finished your points.

## Movement: The Goal Is to Be Like Oprah

One of the great secrets to strong physical presence is moving around your space as you speak. If you can possibly free yourself from the lectern, do it. Move around.

Movement shows confidence, because you're taking

ownership of the space. Look at Oprah – she constantly moves as she presents.

The key to movement is to pick out someone, connect with eye contact, and then close in. You're a homing pigeon, connecting with your listeners and closing in. Each person you close in on will feel special. Do it with enough people during a presentation and you can't lose.

Of course, you don't want to close in so much that you tower over the listener. But get close enough so that they know you're talking to them.

## Keepers

1. If your stance is a handshake, make sure it's a firm and confident one.
2. When presenting, the idea is to be open. When not gesturing, keep your hands open as opposed to closed.
3. Walk around the space as much as possible, connecting with individual audience members and closing in as you speak.

## CHAPTER 18

*"It's connection, not perfection."*
**– Speechworks**

# Inoffensive Gestures

"What do I do with my hands?"

We get that question all the time. We answer with six ways to "be":

**Be** big.

**Be** steady.

**Be** strong.

**Be** forward.

Don't **be** distracting. And finally . . .

Don't **be** too concerned, because gestures don't really matter that much.

## Guess What? Gestures Just Aren't That Important

People tend to be extremely self-conscious about their hands. But the reality is that gestures don't really matter that much. In fact, you can have terrible gestures and still be a great presenter.

Consider Pat Conroy, author of *The Prince of Tides, The Great Santini,* and many others. He has a horribly distracting gesture. When I saw him speak, his glasses didn't fit properly. As a result, he was constantly reaching up and adjusting the frames as they fell down his nose. During a one-hour speech, he probably adjusted his glasses 150 times.

Talk about distracting!

But his gestures didn't matter, because of the passion in his voice and the marvelous stories he told. He is absolutely a wonderful presenter in spite of his less-than-perfect gestures.

So if you're spending a lot of time worrying about your gestures, stop and ask yourself some other questions first. Do I have energy in my voice? Am I making eye contact? Am I smiling? Once you've checked those things off your list, then worry about making sure you have great gestures.

## But Let's Say You Really Want to Perfect Your Gestures: First, Don't Distract

The first lesson in gesturing is the same as the first lesson of being a doctor: "First, do no harm."

Whatever you do with your hands, don't do anything that distracts. For example, don't:
- Jingle your keys.
- Pick your nose or scratch yourself inappropriately (We've seen both).
- Pop your knuckles.
- Present with your arms pinned at your sides like a goofy penguin.
- Have limp "sissy wrists." (A gay client once asked for help with this issue, so don't call me politically incorrect. Do you want people looking at your wrists or listening to your words?)

## And by All Means Avoid the Steve Forbes Bug Release

Steve Forbes, that geekiest of presidential candidates, provided the best example around of a distracting gesture. When I was practicing law, Forbes came to my firm to promote his campaign and ask for money. He stood with his hands clasped in front of him as though he was carefully holding a bunch of bugs, or maybe a little bird.

Here's the weird part. Every time he made a point, he would open his hands like he was releasing that little bird.

So he'd say, "I'd like to tell you my new idea about taxes." And on the word "taxes," he would open his hands and release the bird.

And he made the same gesture with every subsequent point.

"Let me tell you about welfare." And then he'd release the bird.

"Let me tell you about Russia." And then he'd release the bird.

It was highly distracting. I found myself hearing nothing he said, but instead focusing on his hands.

### To Have Good Gestures, Be Like Tiger

Strong gestures are best. Reach out with power.

There are two reasons.

- Strong gestures simply look more confident. Watch an umpire. When he gestures that the runner is out, his gesture is strong so there is no doubt. Your gestures should also be strong.
- Strong gestures add energy to your voice. In our workshops, we have our clients do a Tiger Woods arm pump, complete with a powerful "Yessss!" Then we ask the group to say the same thing but with a slow-motion pump. The "Yessss" always sounds softer and less energetic, demonstrating how weak gestures lead to lower energy in the voice.

### Take That Velcro off Your Elbows: Be Big

Many presenters suffer from a malady we call "Velcro elbows"; they gesture with their elbows held close to their sides. Velcro elbows cause weak, closed-in gestures.

Instead, you want to make big gestures. Reach out toward the listener. Make yourself large. Air out those armpits.

## Keep the Gestures in the Strike Zone

When we tell people to be big, they often will reach way up or way down with their gestures. Generally, however, you want to keep your gestures between the shoulders and the waist.

## When Not Gesturing, Let Your Hands Hang Down at Your Sides

One of the most confident positions a presenter can assume is with her hands at her sides and her weight centered or slightly forward. We call this the neutral stance. So often we want to cover ourselves with our hands, but please try to avoid that urge. Instead, let your hands hang down like a bunch of bananas.

## Get Rid of the Gerbil Arms

Many women suffer from a far worse malady than Velcro elbows: "gerbil arms." They not only clasp their elbows to their body, they hold their wrists up in front of their chest like a gerbil.

This gesturing pattern conveys a sense of weakness.

Fight gerbil arms. Reach out.

## Always Gesture Forward

Gestures should go forward, toward your audience. Think about sports. In virtually every sport, a coach will tell you to keep moving forward. In basketball, you're told to move toward the basket. In soccer, it's move toward the goal.

When presenting, connecting with the audience is your goal. Make sure that your gestures are toward the audience.

## Never Gesture Backwards

Gestures where you reach back look awkward. What happens when you slip on something? You reach backwards, trying to avert a fall. When you gesture backwards, reaching behind you, you look like you're going to fall.

## Don't Be an Apple Picker

Many presenters look like they're picking apples. They reach out and then quickly pull back.

Instead, hold the gesture through a thought.

Remember the home plate umpire calling the sliding player "safe"? His arms reach out and he holds the gesture for a few seconds for emphasis. Imagine how much less impact he would have if he had said "safe" and just flopped his arms out in a halfhearted gesture.

Hold the gesture for emphasis.

## Avoid the Jazz Fingers

Sometimes people have strong gestures otherwise, but hold their hands up like they're playing "patty-cake." If their fingers are splayed, we call this position "jazz fingers."

You want to have your hand extended naturally forward, as if you're reaching out to shake someone's hand.

## Gesturing at the Lectern

When you're at a lectern, you need to raise your gestures up so the audience can see them. When resting your hands, put them high on the lectern, reaching forward. Reaching forward makes your body look three-dimensional. If you drop your hands below the lectern, you look like a talking head.

And don't squeeze the lectern for dear life, as did one presenter we saw. He squeezed so hard that when he was done, he literally picked up the lectern and started to carry it away.

## Keepers

1. Work on your other presentation skills before you worry about your gestures.
2. The first rule of gesturing is don't distract.
3. Good gestures are strong, big, forward, and steady.

## PART III

*"My dad always told me, 'You get out of it what you put into it.'"*

– Tiger Woods

# Getting an A-Game: Some Final Steps for Becoming a Top Geek Communicator

So now you know the Formula and how to craft a message. You also know about the concept of Maximum You and how to come across in a way that connects with listeners.

Now it's time to put it all together into an A-Game. What's an "A-Game"?

It comes from that golf/geek/great Tiger Woods. When Tiger is really playing well, he says, "I had my A-Game today."

As a communicator, you need to have your A-Game every day. This section will show you how to put it all together so that whether you're speaking at a conference, in a meeting, on the telephone, or to venture capitalists, you sound goooooooooooood. You may still be a geek. But you're going to come across as one smooth-talking, listener-focused, easy-to-understand geek. A geek with an A-Game.

## CHAPTER 19

*"Rehearse as if your cash flow depended
on it."*
**– Speechworks**

# Getting Good Takes
Practice

"Aren't great communication and presentation skills really all about
natural ability? Can I really get good at this stuff?"

The answer to that common question brings to mind an old joke.

*Question: How many psychologists does it take to change a
lightbulb?*

*Answer: Only one psychologist. But the lightbulb has to want to
change.*

If you want to be an A-game communicator, you can. Absolutely. The only question is this:

Are you willing to work at it?

To be great, work at specific areas systematically. You will improve quickly. If you work at it long enough, you will become great. Consider the words of Harry Blackstone Jr., the great magician. "Nothing I do can't be done by a 10-year-old . . . with fifteen years of practice." If you focus on improving specific communication skills, you'll be an A-game communicator long before 15 years have passed.

### How Do I Get Good? Pick One or Two Things and Work at Those

Vic Braden, in his classic book *Mental Tennis*, gives a great lesson on how to improve at tennis that applies equally well to communication skills. Here's what he says:

> *When it comes to improvement, most players start thinking in terms of thousands of changes, and of course the whole idea becomes overwhelming. But in fact, frequently all you have to do is solve one or two problems and you become a whole new tennis player. Think about that: If you straighten out one single stroke, you can improve your game enormously.*

The same is true with communication skills. You can dramatically improve the quality of your skills by just improving one or two parts of your overall communications "game."

- Is your biggest problem voice energy? Work on that exclusively until you are able to project Maximum You when you speak.
- Is your problem eye contact? Work on that until you can connect with listeners and build relationships.
- Is your problem poor physical presence? Work on keeping that weight forward and your gestures open.

Solve your biggest problem first, and your ability to communicate will jump significantly.

### An Improvement Plan for 80 Percent of All People, Geeks Included

About 80 percent of the clients who come to our workshops

could catapult themselves from the category of "average communicator" to "A-Game communicator" if they would
commit to do four things.

1. Practice your presentations from beginning to end several
   times.
2. Always begin by telling the listener the big picture, what's
   in it for them.
3. Energize your voice so that you always sound enthusiastic.
4. Smile and make eye contact when you address a person or
   a group. Give 'em the Ol' One-Two.

Just as in tennis, improvements to merely one of these
areas will lift your communications game to the next level. Get
good at all of them and you'll be an A-Game communicator.

## To Be Great, Start by Doing the One Thing That Few People Do: Rehearse

It's no wonder that most people are poor presenters. No one
rehearses.

I met recently with a high-level executive at a major
Internet service provider. He said, "I don't feel I'm very
effective with my presentations."

I asked him the first question I ask anyone who tells me
such things, "How much do you rehearse your presentations?"

His response: "I don't rehearse much. I find it kind of
boring."

My frank response: "Then you have no right to expect to
be effective."

Or, consider a huge computer corporation that was
preparing recently for a major team presentation to introduce
a new software product. Their rehearsal consisted of gather-
ing the team into a conference room and "batting it around"
for an hour or so. They talked about the presentation. They
discussed their introduction and their ending. But they didn't
actually practice getting up and saying the words of the entire
presentation from beginning to end.

Indeed, when I ask people how they rehearse, they
often tell me they "go over it" on the plane heading out to the
meeting location. But that isn't a rehearsal.

You need to rehearse your presentation thoroughly from
beginning to end.

### This May Seem Obvious, but Let's Review What Rehearsal Does for You

1. **Rehearsal prepares your voice to say the right words.** Presenting is a spoken art. Rehearsal gets your mouth used to saying the right words in the right order. When you haven't thoroughly practiced saying the words of your presentation, you will not be confident of the precise way to say everything. For example, a quality assurance manager for an Internet security company worked hard on an analogy for his company's key product. Even though he knew the analogy he wanted to use, it took a good 30 minutes for him to figure out how to say it so that it came out right. If he hadn't rehearsed, he never would have figured out the right way to express his thoughts.

2. **You can focus on the 93 percent.** When you rehearse, you build a level of confidence in your material that allows you to stop worrying about the substance and focus on delivering the speech with energy, eye contact, and good physical presence. Remember, it's just as important to look and sound confident as to be right.

3. **You learn your time limit.** Only when you rehearse will you truly get a sense of the length of your presentation.

### An Extra Warning on Time Limits

In the Speechworks Code of Crimes Against Audiences, speaking beyond your time limit during a presentation is a crime punishable by hanging, firing squad, electrocution, lethal injection, or even being drawn and quartered.

At the very least, someone should give you a Bronx cheer.

If you have 20 minutes to speak, don't ever, ever, under any circumstances speak for 21 minutes. The best presenters will speak for 15 minutes and leave five minutes for questions.

Don't you feel abused by presenters who go beyond their allotted time? Of course you do. Why don't you get up to leave? Because like most people, you're too polite. But while you may be sitting politely, you're steaming inside because the dope at the lectern didn't have the discipline to rehearse his presentation a few times with a stopwatch.

## To Improve Specific Skills, Employ Reticular Activation

One of the greatest tools available for improving communication skills is something called "reticular activation."

Reticular activation is the little bug we plant in our heads to sensitize ourselves to certain things. For example, reticular activation is what makes you suddenly begin to notice all the blue Toyota Camrys on the road two days after you've bought your first Camry. There aren't any more Camrys on the road, but your brain is suddenly sensitized to them.

You can use reticular activation to change and improve your communication habits. You simply need to plant in your head a bug to improve the key item. Write down what you want to improve at the beginning of every day.

Recently, I heard a media guru speak to a convention hall filled with (by my estimate) about 3,000 people. He had one hour to speak. Amazingly, he wasn't able to say everything in an hour. He rambled through some interesting observations and the occasional entertaining anecdote. But to my great dismay, toward the end, he said, "I know I'm out of time, but let me add just a few things." He then spoke for 10 more minutes.

My first thought was, "Good heavens! If you can't say it in an hour, you should seek professional help." Then I did a quick calculation on the back of an envelope. His lack of discipline in preparing his presentation had wasted 10 minutes for every one of the 3,000 people in the convention hall. That works out to a total of almost three weeks of wasted time.

Give that media geek a wedgie.

- **Want to improve your posture?** Sensitize your brain to check yourself out in the mirrored elevator doors or the store windows as you're walking down the street. Are you standing with your shoulders back and weight forward?
- **Want to learn to improve your gestures?** Write down that you need to make big gestures and hold those gestures through a thought as you speak. Or you may want to put a sticky note on your telephone to remind yourself to stand and gesture as you talk on conference calls.

- **Want to remember to smile?** Tell your brain to remember to smile as you speak. Do like the best telemarketers do, and put a mirror on your desk to make sure you're smiling while you talk into the telephone. The listener on the other end of the line may not be able to see the smile, but they sure can hear it.
- **Voice energy an issue?** Put sticky notes everywhere to remind yourself to be Maximum You.

### Some Advice from Benjamin Franklin

Benjamin Franklin probably didn't know the term *reticular activation*. But he certainly understood the concept. After some experimentation, Franklin learned that it took 21 days to change a habit. He'd pick one thing he wanted to change and work on it every day for three weeks straight. Then he'd pick something else.

So take a tip from one of the Founding Fathers: pick one thing you want to work on and focus on it for 21 days.

Before you know it, you'll no longer be using those annoying filler words and you'll be able to begin working on gestures.

### A Final Thought on Improving Your Communication Skills: This Ain't a Mystery, It's as Easy as Working Hard

Despite what many communications gurus want you to think, becoming an A-Game communicator is not mysterious. You don't need to practice any sort of meditation to get in touch with your inner self. You don't need to practice special breathing techniques. You don't need some jerk to humiliate you because you have a soft voice.

Getting good at communicating is really quite simple.

But it isn't easy.

It's like golf. Getting good at golf is a simple process that everyone understands. You must go to the driving range and hit 500 shots a day for several years in a row. Then go to the practice green and putt a couple hundred seven-footers a day for several years in a row. Then practice those chips, a couple hundred at a time, every day for several years.

Nothing complicated. It just takes work.

Similarly, improving your communication skills is no

mystery. You need to work hard at projecting energy and enthusiasm. You need to work hard at remembering to smile when you speak. You need to work hard at remembering to focus on the listener's interests.

It's simple. You just have to work hard.

## Keepers

1. You can become a great presenter if you want to work at it.
2. Work at each piece of your presentation "game" for 21 days until you've gotten that piece to the level you want. Then move to another piece.
3. Rehearse, rehearse, rehearse.

## CHAPTER 20

*"Success is the old ABCs – ability . . .*
*breaks . . . courage."*
**– Unknown**

# Stepping It Up to the Next Level: Interactive Presenting

Three geeks. Three interactive presentations. Three involved, engaged audiences.

- A document management software sales rep goes to a big sales presentation. Rather than whip out a PowerPoint projector, he pulls out a marker and approaches the whiteboard. "Let's start by brainstorming all the ways that you're dissatisfied with how you produce forms from your current software."

- Asked to speak on administrative motion practice (ouch), a lawyer gives his audience a series of hypotheticals starring Homer Simpson to resolve in discussion groups.
- An accountant explains a new accounting regulation, but stops after every major point to answer questions, rather than waiting until the end.

Regardless of your skill as a communicator, there is one easy way to virtually guarantee that your audience will benefit from and enjoy your presentation: Make the presentation interactive. Any good A-game communicator appreciates what an edge an interactive presentation can give you in certain situations.

## What Is an Interactive Presentation?

In interactive presentations, audience participation is a planned, integral part of the program and not merely an afterthought.

Interactive presentations:
- Plan for and encourage questions from the audience.
- Allow the audience to brainstorm answers to questions from the presenter.
- Present the audience with problems to be solved using the principles discussed by the presenter.
- Give the audience exercises that illustrate the speaker's points.

## Why Do Interactive Presentations Work So Well? Let Us Count the Ways.

Interactive presentations ensure that listeners get answers to their important questions.

Because the audience participates, they take some responsibility for the content, ensuring that they will get the information they want.

Consider a large provider of telephone equipment that was having trouble with hostile reactions from certain prospective clientele. The cause of the hostility was that the equipment provider had obtained a near monopoly position on some critical equipment.

Their clients didn't like being so dependent on a single supplier. It turned out that the equipment provider allowed very little time for questions during their presentations. The effect was that they came across as arrogant and not interested in their client's concerns.

By adding substantial time for questions during the presentations, their clients had opportunity to vent and be comfortable that their concerns were being properly handled.

**Interactive is more persuasive.**
Bob Pike, the training guru and author, points out that "People don't argue with their own data." That statement has a huge implication for your presentations. It means that to the extent you can involve the audience's experiences in supporting your arguments, you will not only have a fully engaged audience, you will have a more fully persuaded audience.

For example, the American Society of Training and Development recently did a survey to determine the most important characteristics in a business leader. One way to present the information would be to simply read the results of the survey to the audience.

But what would happen if, instead, you asked the audience to list what they thought were the most important characteristics? Chances are that they'd list most of the key factors determined by ASTD. More importantly, the listeners would be inclined to believe the information since they generated it themselves.

And if they happened to leave off a few key points, you could simply add them to the list, citing the ASTD survey.

**Interactive teaches better.**
Confucius said, "What I hear, I forget; What I see, I remember; What I do, I understand." Once again, this principle has a huge implication for creating presentations that have impact.

Sure, you could lecture an audience for two hours about a new accounting regulation. Would they remember what you said? Maybe they'd remember some things. But they wouldn't remember much.

What if you did what a top accounting firm did when a new regulation came out? They had several of their key customers in and actually gave them some hypothetical accounting problems to solve using the new regulations.

The presentation had more impact because the audience was actively involved in learning the information.

**Interactive presentations are more fun for the listener and usually less work for the presenter.**
The word "lecture" these days has become synonymous with "boring." That's because most lectures are boring and a tad condescending. Audience involvement creates a fun atmosphere and eliminates the stuffy feel of most presentations.

Consider the lawyer who was tasked with putting together a presentation for a bunch of administrative law judges on a new set of procedural rules. The judges had allotted three hours for the talk.

Three hours!

Think about how much work it would have been to write a three-hour lecture! Ugh.

Instead, the lawyer spoke for only about half an hour. The rest of the time, he allowed the judges to team up into small groups and work their way through a series of hypothetical scenarios starring the cartoon character Homer Simpson.

Each group then chose a "captain" to report on their conclusions. The lawyer leading the session had a few key points to make about each hypothetical, which he brought up after the team had given its report.

The judges loved it and learned a lot, far more than they would have had they been forced to sit through a three-hour lecture.

### Why Presenters Aren't More Interactive
**Ego.** Let's face it, folks. Few things sound better than hearing your own voice. I mean, it sounds sooooo good. The same is true, however, for the listener. They love hearing their own voices as well. And who is the presentation for? The listener. So why not make the listeners the center of the presentation? Let them speak. They're dying to say something.

**Fear of loss of control.** Most presenters don't have enough confidence to allow the audience loose – they fear losing control. "What if they ask questions I can't answer?" "What if I can't get control of the room?" To give an effective interactive presentation, you certainly have to know your information cold. You need to spend a lot less time organizing your speech and more time planning responses to questions. But if you let the audience in on the fun, you'll be surprised at the rewards.

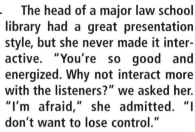

The head of a major law school library had a great presentation style, but she never made it interactive. "You're so good and energized. Why not interact more with the listeners?" we asked her. "I'm afraid," she admitted. "I don't want to lose control."

A year later, we heard her again and she started her presentation by getting the audience to respond to some questions. Meanwhile she had cut back her remarks substantially. When we complimented her, she responded, "I'm working at it and the audiences seem more captivated."

## How to Make Your Presentations More Interactive

**Factor question-and-answer sessions into your presentation.** This is the simplest and often most effective way to make a program more interactive and fun. At the end of every major point, throw open the floor for questions. If they don't ask anything at first, as I've suggested before, you could say, "One of the first questions people usually ask is. . . ." That typically gets them going.

**Kick off the presentation with an icebreaker.** A stockbroker we work with gives investment seminars to the public. Rather than starting with a lecture, he begins with a flip chart and asks everyone to list the financial bases they need to have covered before they can invest in the stock market.

**Have a brainstorming session of the key issues facing your department and then prioritize the most important issues to the group.**

**Have discussion groups and let a group member report on the key findings.**

Before sending smaller groups off to discuss something on their own, be sure they have enough information to have a satisfactory discussion. For example, if you want them to solve a business problem, be sure they have all the facts necessary to solve that problem.

## Keepers

1. Interactive presentations are more fun for the audience, more persuasive, and easier to prepare.
2. Making a presentation interactive will enable your listeners to learn and retain the information better than if you lecture.
3. Lots of question-and-answer time is the simplest way to make a presentation interactive.

## CHAPTER 21

*"Life is not a rehearsal."*
**– Unknown**

# The Thirty-Second Elevator Pitch

One of the worst elevator speeches ever came from a software engineer who was asked by a CEO what he did for a living.

The answer: "I do 802.11."

Huh?

An elevator speech is a thirty-second conversation starter that tells people what you do in a way that focuses on the listener's interest. A-Game communicators always have a good elevator pitch. The goal of any elevator pitch can vary. The classic elevator speech is a sales tool, designed to entice the listener into wanting to know more and eventually pulling them into the sales cycle. You may, however, simply want to be able to articulate your job in a way that connects with your conversation partner to get the discussion going.

By any standard, however, "I do 802.11" doesn't cut it.

## Writing an Elevator Pitch

Coming up with your elevator pitch resembles writing a presentation. You need to start with an understanding of your goal and an understanding of your listener's interests. Bring those two together, and throw in a piece of evidence that illustrates what you do, and you've got an elevator pitch.

## Elevator Pitch to Investors

What do investors want? They want chances to get rich, or should I say rich-er. With that in mind, your elevator pitch to an investor has to give a taste of how you're going to make lots of money.

Consider a high-tech firm that made a special type of cable modem. This modem was capable of taking a regular television cable in one end and putting out both cable and telephone lines on the other end. In other words, it could turn a cable company into a cable/telephone company. Revolutionary stuff.

When asked what they do, their chief marketing officer said, "We sell cable modems." Obviously, this was not a marketing officer interested in getting rich any time soon.

Instead, they should focus on giving the investor a sense of the huge opportunity for making a lot of money. How about . . .

*We're revolutionizing the cable industry with a patented piece of technology that can turn companies like Time Warner, normally a cable company, into a telephone company as well. The technology is a cable modem that sits beside your TV. It takes in the TV cable on one end and puts out both a TV cable and several telephone lines.*

After hearing that, any investor worth her millions will be seeing dollar signs.

### Elevator Pitch to Prospects

What is a sales prospect interested in? Solutions to problems. With that in mind, your elevator pitch to a sales prospect should highlight how your product serves or solves your client's problems.

Bill Marianes is a transactional attorney with the law firm Troutman Sanders in Atlanta. When people ask him what he does for a living, he says, "I'm a problem solver and dream facilitator." That's appropriate, because when people come to see a lawyer, he says, they either have a problem or something they want to accomplish. After hearing the Marianes elevator pitch, prospective clients are always lured into asking him more detail about what he does.

He never responds to the question, "What do you do?" with "I'm an attorney." That kind of response, he says, means, "I'm stuck with whatever box they put all the attorneys and lawyers in. I don't have a chance to distinguish myself."

Here's the Speechworks elevator speech:

*We are a presentation and communication training company. We do two basic things. We teach you how to put together a presentation that wins business and motivates listeners. We then teach you how to deliver that message so that you form relationships with your listeners.*

### Elevator Pitch at a Cocktail Party

Say all you want to do is have a decent conversation starter at a cocktail party, something a little catchier than "We do 802.11." Once again, you need to focus on what about your work will be of interest to your listener. I have a friend who works for a large electric utility. When people ask what he does for a living, he has a carefully considered response. He doesn't say, "I help my company in regulatory proceedings before state and federal agencies." Snore.

Instead, he focuses his response on what he knows will interest his listener. "You know that electric bill you pay every month? I work to set the electric rates that determine the amount of that bill."

### Do You Talk to Your Mother with That Mouth? What an Elevator Pitch Is Not!

When writing an elevator pitch, remember that it will come out of your mouth. So it better sound like something you'd actually say. Too often, companies construct elaborate elevator pitches that sound like marketing brochure copy. But when you try to say them, you sound like a freak.

Here's an "elevator pitch" that one e-business came up with after paying a lot of money to a Silicon Valley marketing guru.

*We deliver easy-to-implement e-business solutions from the Web site to your loading dock to your customer's mailbox. Our unparalleled breadth of expertise provides fully maximized solutions to overcome ever-increasing global e-business demands, customer satisfaction, and competitive superiority.*

O.K., sure it says a lot. And it passes the requirement that it generates conversation. But what kind of conversation? Who talks like that? If someone said that to me in an elevator, I'd be getting off on the next floor.

Make sure that your elevator pitch sounds right coming out of your mouth. Play it back on a tape recorder. If it sounds good, then it's your pitch.

Three masons were working on a cathedral in New York City. A little girl approaches the first and says, "What are you doing?"

The first mason replies, "Well, I take that sand and mix it in this bucket to make the cement."

When she asks the second mason the same question, he replies, "My job is to take this load of bricks and stack them together to form a wall."

When she asks the third mason the question, he puts down his trowel, looks the little girl in the eye, and says, "I'm building a cathedral."

Give the third mason a raise for his great elevator pitch.

### Delivering the Elevator Pitch: Practice, Practice, Practice

Now that you've got your elevator pitch, what are you going to do with it? You need to take it for a test drive.

Practice saying it.

Remember that communication is a spoken art. Your elevator pitch needs to flow out of your mouth spontaneously.

One large computer firm prepared for a convention by having all the engineers attending the convention pair up and practice giving the pitch to one another. They did it five times each so that the words flowed.

You need to know it so well that you can deliver it with

- Voice energy
- Eye contact
- A smile

## Follow Up with a Question

So you've wowed them with your great elevator speech. What do you do now?

Ask your listener a question such as, "So, what do YOU do?"

The goal of an elevator pitch is to pique a listener's interest and get a conversation going. If it's a potential client, a question will help qualify the prospect. If you're just schmoozing, asking questions of people gets them talking about their favorite topic: themselves.

## Keepers

1. An elevator pitch briefly tells what you do in a way that is of interest to your listener.
2. Make sure that your elevator pitch sounds like something you'd actually say. You don't want it to sound like marketing brochure copy.
3. Practice your elevator pitch.

*"You have the will to win. But do you have the will to prepare?"*

**– Bill Curry, football coach/broadcaster**

# How to Get Millions of Dollars: Pitching to Venture Capitalists

A little something to bear in mind when you're pitching your get-rich idea to venture capitalists: They're already rich!

But they want more. And your goal, during your 10- to 20-minute pitch, must be to capture their imagination with visions of even-greater wealth and excitement. You need to make them see how you and your team can deliver the next "new new thing." And never is it more important for a geek to have his A-Game as a communicator than when he is asking for $10 million.

### Required Elements of a Venture Capital Pitch

A venture capital presentation has some required elements, all of which help the venture capitalist judge whether or not to give you millions of dollars. Every presentation must have descriptions of:

- The market need your product or service fills ("My software solves all parking problems at the nation's airports at no cost to taxpayers").
- Your management team (the venture capitalists are betting on your team more than your idea).
- How the idea will make money ("Each piece of software will go for $200,000"). This section should include results of any trials you have done.
- How much money you expect to make ("We see 100,000 businesses needing this software"). Venture capitalists call this "the size of the opportunity."
- Proprietary technology to help you capture your market ("We own the patented technology that is the only solution to this problem").

As much as possible, every venture capitalist presentation needs to touch on these topics to some degree.

### The Speechworks Formula as Applied to a Venture Capital Presentation

The Formula works beautifully when asking for huge sums of money from venture capitalists.

### The Message Objective of a Venture Capital Pitch: Tell Them They Have a Chance to Be a Part of Something Exciting

Like any Message Objective, your MO to a venture capitalist brings together what you want (money) with what's in it for them. Your MO should focus on getting the venture capitalist excited about what they could get out of the investment. It should sound something like this:

*"If you invest in this product, you will be getting in on the ground floor of a technological breakthrough that will revolutionize the computing field and make us all wildly rich."* (You can leave off the "wildly rich" stuff if you are pretty sure they'll get the idea.)

## No More Than Three Points: Venture Capitalists Like Tight Presentations, Too

Even though venture capital pitches have several required elements, you can fit it all into three big points.
- What we want to do.
- How we are the right ones to do it.
- Why we expect to make a lot of money.

### 1. What We Want to Do.
- **Go into detail about your product.** For example, Netuitive, an Atlanta software start-up, explained how their product would enable Web site owners to predict short-term spikes in Web site usage, something that previously had been virtually impossible.
- **Any trials you've already done showing that your idea works.** Netuitive explained that they had already tried their technology in the electric utility industry and it was a success.
- **Discuss whether your technology is proprietary.** One of the first things a venture capitalist will want to know is whether you have exclusive use of a particular product. Netuitive explained that the key patented technology was called the Adaptive Correlation Engine.
- **Discuss your business model.** "We intend to make money by charging $200,000 for each copy of our software."

### 2. How We Are the Right Ones to Do It.
- **Discuss your management team.** Every venture capital presentation must explain why the venture capitalists should invest in you. When eGulliver was pitching for funds for its travel site, Deslie Webb detailed how she and her team all came from a major travel agent. This signaled that they clearly knew their business.
- **Discuss any prior investors you've had.** Showing who has invested so far is another way of demonstrating your bona fides to the world.
- **Tell a little about your background if it's impressive.** For example, Buck Goldstein, whose venture capital firm NetWorth invests in high-tech ventures, said he found himself persuaded and liking one entrepreneur who wanted to

take his interest in recycling onto the Internet. During the proposal, the person explained that he had had a recycling business in the past, but saw many problems with the business as it currently was practiced. So he persuaded a high-level executive at Georgia Pacific to quit his job and join him in a new Internet recycling venture. Goldstein found this personal story persuasive, and it helped make him comfortable that this person might make a good long-term business partner.

### 3. Why We Expect to Make a Lot of Money.

- **Discuss the financial projections.** Netuitive included a spreadsheet showing how many customers they expected to have, along with the total income they expected.
- **Discuss plans to market the product.** Netuitive detailed how it planned to market its software, among other things, through partnerships with large consulting firms that were in the business of installing and managing Internet software applications.
- **Try to figure out the size of the "opportunity."** This is where you want to try and make their mouths water. How many potential buyers for your product exist? What is the size of the market? When Healtheon was wooing investors in its early stages, CEO Mike Long argued that the company was positioned to become a major player in the $1.5 trillion-a-year health care industry. He would explain to investors that there are 700,000 doctors in the U.S. alone, and Healtheon expected to sign up 500,000 of them at an annual cost of $20,000 a year to enable them to conduct their business over the Internet. Then Long would step back and say, "You do the math."
- **Don't be shy.** One entrepreneur we spoke to tells the story of preparing for his second round of funding. He goes to his current investors with his pitch. When they see his financial projections, they are appalled. "You need to double those projections," he is told. Obviously, you shouldn't lie about your projections – but remember that these investors are already millionaires. They probably won't invest unless they see a chance to become gazillionaires. So don't be modest about your projected earnings.

## The Hook: Paint a Picture of Your Product Saving the World

A classic way to begin a venture capital presentation is with a quick story that illustrates the market problem your product solves. This approach almost always works. Here's how Anindya Datta, CEO of Chutney, opened a presentation at a recent conference of venture capitalists.

*"Imagine Bob, the e-shopper. Bob likes to read. He regularly visits Papyrus.com, an online bookseller. Papyrus.com tracks Bob's clicks as he navigates through the site. Let's say Bob enters the Papyrus site at the home page, and then navigates the following link path: Fiction – Thriller – Legal Thriller. Let us now assume that people who follow the Fiction – Thriller – Legal Thriller path are known to be interested in fusion jazz. This type of knowledge is widely mined by sites these days. Wouldn't it be cool to be able to present Bob, right at that moment, with an e-coupon from Tower Records with a special discount for titles in the fusion jazz category? This is extremely hard to do."*

Anindya then went on to explain how his company has proprietary technology to do just that.

Or consider how Netuitive began one of its venture capital pitches. Bob Zack, the company president, began as follows:

*"If you went to the Toys'R'Us Web site last Christmas, you would have seen a message from the company to its customers. That message would have explained how any toys purchased after early December would not be shipped out by Christmas. As a result of the problems Toys'R'Us had with its Web site, the company had to ship gift certificates to its customers to allow them to go to the company's stores to buy gifts prior to Christmas. Now if Toys'R'Us had been using the Netuitive technology to monitor and predict usage on their Web site, they may have been able to avoid much of the nightmare they experienced last Christmas."*

Bob Zack then went on to explain how Netuitive has a software application that enables Web sites to predict short-term fluctuations and spikes in usage that, if unforeseen, can cripple an Internet e-tailer like Toys'R'Us.

## Wrap: This Is Not the Time to Be Bashful. Ask for the Dough.

At the end of a venture capital presentation, it's important to straightforwardly ask for what you want. Let's be clear about this: If you want $15 million to take your product to market, you need to say, "We want $15 million to take our product to market over the next year. In exchange for that funding, you will receive the opportunity to make 20 times your investment in the next two years."

## An Interview with an Investment Banker on Geek Speakers

*Brian Sadler does regular lunches with high-tech entrepreneurs. As managing director of Legacy Securities, an Atlanta investment bank specializing in entrepreneurial and middle-market companies, those lunches are part of his job. He works closely with such entrepreneurs to help them raise funds for their businesses. But by the time the check arrives, Sadler has usually become frustrated. To hear him tell it, it's rare to find someone who can succinctly express their business idea so that he, a banker of above-average intelligence, can understand. We asked him what it was like listening to geeks pitch their ideas.*

**Q: Tell me what it's normally like when you sit down to talk with a high-tech entrepreneur pitching his idea.**

I'll give somebody an hour. The first thing I'll say is, "Tell me about your business. Give me the 30-second overview." Because if you don't start framing immediately how to communicate the idea, they'll talk to you for a couple of hours and you won't know what they do.

**Q: Give me an example.**

I met recently with a researcher/scientist. He was going out on his own and he had some technology related to telecommunications. And he has a model and he wants to commercialize it. We go over to lunch at The Palm across the street. I say "O.K., explain this to me." He says, "Well, it does kinda sorta this. And I got these patents. And I got this and I got that." He keeps talking and he's hitting me literally in the first minute or two with 20 or 30 ideas, none of them capturing what it is he wants to do. Eventually, I have to inter-rupt him, because after 10 minutes I'm not listening. I'm getting frustrated. My blood pressure's going up. I'm think-ing, "It's going to be another one of those days." So I interrupt him and I say, "Let's just step back. Can you give me just the best picture in 30 seconds of exactly what it is you're doing?"

He literally couldn't do it. He started talking again. Five minutes later I still don't know what he does. So then I start-ed asking him a set of questions. I said, "Is it hardware or software?" He wasn't even explaining it well enough for me to understand that. He said, "Well, it's kind of a combination of both." I said, "Well, does the hardware exist today?" He said, "Well, the hardware's kind of there. But I'll want a manufacturer to make some new hardware." I said, "And what about the software?" He said, "Well, the software is this, best of breed, best of breed." I said, "It looks to me like most of what you're talking about is technology that is already there, but you're going to apply the technology in a new way." "Well, yeah," he said. "That's exactly it. It's no new technology. It's an application." Now that's important for me to understand, whether it's applying somebody else's technology or am I creating something new.

## Q: What happened with this fellow?

Any person where it takes an hour to explain their thing and I have to hold their hand like that, well, it's going to be too dif-ficult for me to work with them. This guy will fail. It doesn't mean that the business couldn't work. But he will never suc-ceed because he cannot communicate to another human being what his idea is. Yeah, with time you can figure it out. I fig-ured it out. But with a guy like that, anybody on the other side of the table is going think he's a big old tekkie nerd who can't communicate.

## Be Sure You Present Yourself as Someone They'd Like to Work with: Don't Ignore Style Issues

Many entrepreneurs make the mistake of putting all their energy into writing a presentation, but none into practicing, working on their style, and making it "sing."

Mistake! Be sure to spend enough time practicing that you can inject plenty of voice energy, eye contact, and smiles. Venture capitalists aren't just looking for an investment; they're looking for a business partner. "You invest in people you like to spend time with," said Buck Goldstein of NetWorth. "To some extent, we're judging the entrepreneur first and the business second."

With that in mind, venture capitalists look for entrepreneurs who can present themselves well and connect with their listeners. "It doesn't matter how good your business plan is if you don't establish a mutual trust and rapport," said Ed Croft, of the Atlanta investment banking firm Croft and Bender.

What does this all add up to?

Rehearse your presentation repeatedly so that you'll be able to focus on the presentation skills and not just the content. You want to make eye contact. "They don't want someone that won't look 'em in the eye," said Croft.

You want to have strong voice energy. You want to smile. Think about it. Be the person that you'd consider giving $1 million.

### Question and Answer: Maybe the Most Important Part of a Venture Capital Presentation

Perhaps the most important part of any venture capital presentation is preparing for questions. We worked recently with an entrepreneur who stood to give a well-rehearsed presentation. But no sooner had he begun than the venture capitalist started peppering him with questions.

He hardly got to deliver any of his prepared pitch.

Good thing he had spent some time brainstorming on the possible questions. Otherwise, he'd have seemed ill prepared.

### Keepers

1. Follow the Speechworks Formula for a venture capital presentation.
2. Rehearse repeatedly so that you'll be able to pitch with energy and eye contact. Build rapport.
3. Prepare for questions and answers.

## CHAPTER 23

*"Getting people to like you is the other side of liking them."*
– **Norman Vincent Peale**

# Schmoozing for Geeks: How to Connect at Networking Functions

Want new friends? Want to make connections for business?

Learn to schmooze. Anyone can do it. You just need to learn three things.

- The schmoozing mind-set of showing curiosity about others.
- How to remember names.
- The keys to working a room.

Once again, A-Game communicators schmooze with the best.

### The Schmoozing Mind-set: Show Interest in Others

Here's a conversation I've had numerous times with my wife as we're driving home from a party.

*Me:* I met Bob Smith, a senior product manager of Widget Corporation.

*Johanna:* What did you talk about?

*Me:* Well, he told me all about his latest project. They're rolling out a new line of widgets. This new widget will beat the old widgets in dozens of ways. They expect to stomp the competition. Guess how many questions he asked about my business.

*Johanna:* Not a single question.

*Me:* Not a single question.

Unfortunately, Bob is a typical corporate geek. He is so wrapped up in his own work that he shows little interest in anything outside his field. This is not to say that he is a bad person. He just doesn't realize the one true rule of schmoozing: **the way to schmooze is to show interest in other people and ask them questions.**

### Why Does This Work?

People like people who show interest in them.
　　Any questions?
　　I didn't think so.

### Old MacDonald Had a Farm, E-I-O

Here's a little device that should help you remember the kinds of questions to ask when you're in a schmoozing situation. Remember the nursery rhyme about Old MacDonald? Keep the letters "E-I-O" in your head.

　　**E stands for Experiences.** Ask your conversation partner about his experiences at his current job. Or about her experiences on her recent trip to China.

　　**I stands for Interests.** "So what about your job is most interesting to you?"

**O stands for Opinions.** "Tell me what you think about. . . ."

## And Listen to the Answers

Of course, you need to continue the conversation by listening carefully to the answers and following up. Again, show real interest. Truman Capote may have been the best schmoozer ever because he loved to listen, even to the most boring people. After all, he wondered with fascination, what makes them so boring?

## Learn to Remember Names: It's Not as Hard as You Think, If You Make It a Hobby

One of the true characteristics of a great schmoozer is the ability to remember people's names. What sounds better to a person than her own name? Nothing. Learn to remember names, and that alone will make you a darned good schmoozer.

After years of never being able to recall names, I decided a year ago that I was going to become great at remembering them. And one year later I'm darned good at it. I can remember the names of almost everyone I meet at a party. I know the names of everyone on my street and at work. When I give presentations, I can remember the names of as many as 20 people in the audience, an incredibly valuable tool in getting a crowd to warm up to you. I have no trouble remembering the names of all the parents in my kids' Cub Scout troops, and so on.

How did I do it? It wasn't hard. I just made remembering names my hobby. By that I mean I studied the process of remembering names, read several books about it, and tried out several theories.

## Three-Step Name Recall Process

Anyone who is good at remembering names does three things.

1. They listen to the name when they first hear it.
2. They use one of several name recall systems.
3. They take special care to remember the names of their "life communities."

## Be Alert to the Name When You Hear It

Any book you read on remembering names will tell you the

same thing about why most people are terrible at remembering names: they never listen to a person's name in the first place.

Sure, you hear the name. But do you listen carefully and take it in? Do you make a point to hear it? Do you ask whether you're pronouncing it right? Do you repeat it back to the person? Do you use it immediately when talking to the person?

When I was first trying to remember people's names, I found that simply listening carefully to the name when I heard it made me remember the names of half the people I met.

## Name Recall Systems: All Work, but One Is More Practical Than the Others

I know of three name recall systems. I know that all three work. But to my mind, only one is really practical. So I'll start with that one.

### Periodic self-testing

I use a method that I developed myself. After listening carefully to get a person's name, I self-test myself on people's names throughout an event.

For example, let's say I meet three people at once: Bob, Sarah, and Jim. After listening carefully to their names, I self-test myself as we make small talk. As we're in our little chatting group, I'll look at each of their faces and say, "That's Jim. That's Bob. That's Sarah." I'll do it a couple of times in different orders.

Then, every time I see them, even if I'm just walking by myself to the bar, I'll say, "Hi, Sarah" out loud or to myself. If I see a group of people across the room that I've met, I will test myself on all of their names.

If I find that I have forgotten a person's name, I'll listen to hear another introduction. Or next time I see them I'll simply say, "I'm sorry, tell me your name again."

While I find that I do remember many of the names for a long time (i.e., the next time I see those people), I will also self-test myself the next day or even the next week on specific names that I want to be sure not to forget.

### Writing the names down

Some books will tell you to write down the names in a little book and review the names periodically. This certainly works, but who is going to do that for any length of time?

I tried it for about a week and gave up.

### Use goofy mnemonic devices

Harry Lorayne, the magician, author, and memory expert, used to do a trick where he would greet every member of an audience as they came into an auditorium. At some point, he'd have all 400 people stand up. Then, he'd call their names out one at a time, telling them to sit down.

The trick was pure memory. He explains how he was able to do it in his book *The Memory Book*. When he would meet someone, he'd associate the name with something distinctive about that person's face. For example, if the person's name was Jim and he had a giant nose, Lorayne would imagine that the man's nose was a jungle gym.

I found this technique too hard. I would spend lots of time trying to figure out images to go with a person's name. I must admit, however, that if you can come up with the images, the system works.

### Learn the Names of People in Your Life Communities

I find that you will get the most value out of remembering names if you simply commit to remembering the people in your "life communities." By life communities, I mean those groups of people you know you're going to see again. For example, you can spend extra time remembering the names of all the people at your company, on your street, at your place of worship, on your child's soccer team.

When I was practicing law, I would periodically go through the office directory to make sure I knew the names of everyone in the company. Most "life communities" have similar directories. There's no reason that you can't go through them periodically and test yourself on the names. Then, next time you see Frank after church, you'll know his name and he'll feel great.

## Know How to Work a Room

If you ask lots of questions of people and learn to remember their names, you're going to be a good schmoozer. But there are a few do's and don'ts for working a room that you should keep in mind.

**Be up.** Be Maximum You when you're at a networking function or a party. No one wants to be around someone who is not up.

**Don't head straight for the food table.** Work the room a little before you grab a plate of shrimp.

**Smile and stick your hand out** and introduce yourself to people who are not already engaged in conversation.

**Put your name tag on your right side.** It's easier for people to read it while they're shaking your right hand.

**If you suspect that the other person may not remember your name,** don't say, "I bet you don't remember me." Instead, stick your hand out and say, "Bob, Joey Asher, good to see you again."

**Think of conversation topics on your way to the party.** If something interesting has just happened in the news, prepare a question or two to use to start a discussion. When *Who Wants to Marry a Multimillionaire?* was the media topic of the week, I asked people if they had seen the show and what they thought of it. Everyone had an opinion on the topic.

## Keepers

1. Show interest in others by asking questions.
2. Learn to remember names.
3. Learn the keys to working a room.

# A Final Geeky
# Thought

In my law school, there was a professor who used to survey the lecture hall and affix his gaze on some poor unsuspecting law student ("law student" is another synonym for geek). "Please recite for us the facts of the case of *Pennoyer v. Neff*," this professor would say, knowing that the poor student was looking to escape through a trap door (or maybe it was just me who felt that way). As the poor law student sweated, the professor would then lay on a little bit of extra pressure by saying, "This is an important case. What you say is important. **Please dare to be great."**

I confess that I don't recall much about *Pennoyer v. Neff* (other than it's apparently an important case). But "dare to be great" has always stuck with me as a piece of advice worth remembering. To be a great communicator, you need to **dare.** You need to dare to be Maximum You. You need to dare to focus primarily on your listener's issues and ask directly for the order. You need to dare to allow your audience to ask questions, even if it means giving up a little control of the presentation.

Indeed, if you dare to take the many ideas presented throughout this book to heart, and practice them every day, you can be great. It's within your grasp, I promise you. You can be a geek who's also a great communicator.

A geek with an A-game! Now that's a hard combination to beat.

**Joey Asher** is president of Speechworks. As a presentation and communication consultant, he has coached executives, managers, and sales professionals at Equifax, Compaq, UPS, Scientific Atlanta, Worldcom, and many others. Prior to being a consultant, Joey worked as a newspaper reporter for the Gannett newspaper chain in Georgia and New York. He worked as an adjunct professor of law at Emory University School of Law and was an attorney at Troutman Sanders L.L.P. in Atlanta.

Asher is also the author of *Selling & Communication Skills for Lawyers*, published by American Lawyer Media, 2005. To learn more about Speechworks, visit our website at: www.speechworks.net.